The Ribbon at Olympia's Throat

SEMIOTEXT(E) NATIVE AGENTS SERIES

Originally published as *Le ruban au cou d'Olympia*.
© Editions GALLIMARD, 1981.

Published by Semiotext(e)
PO BOX 629, South Pasadena, CA 91031
www.semiotexte.com

Cover Art: Édouard Manet, *Olympia* (detail). 1863. Oil on canvas, 130.5 x 190 cm. Photo: Patrice Schmidt. Musee d'Orsay
© RMN-Grand Palais / Art Resource, NY

Author photograph: Edward Quinn © edwardquinn.com
Design: Hedi El Kholti
ISBN: 978-1-63590-084-2

Distributed by The MIT Press, Cambridge, Mass. and London, England
Printed in the United States of America

Michel Leiris

The Ribbon at Olympia's Throat

Translated by Christine Pichini

Foreword by Marc Augé

‹e›

Leiris and Olympia: *Modernité, merdonité*[1]

The Ribbon at Olympia's Throat begins with the evocation of a dizzy spell that reminds Leiris of the proximity of death, but reassures him in a way: perhaps he could take that step he so dreads taking "in the blink of an eye." The specter of that moment is always present within him from then on; he writes, he admits, to defend "against the idea of death." For the idea of death is intolerable, as it refers to the idea of nothingness, the fatal culmination of the sequence of "before" and "after" that creates history until the moment when every reference to identity is abolished.

Art and writing, from this perspective, are above all signs of life, as long as they express something of their era, succeed in being "contemporary," which means, if we think about it, being social. For as we know from common experience, no "individual" identity exists without (social) relations; the experience of psychoanalysis and the contributions of ethnology confirm it, if there were any need to. Art and writing are not only signs of personal identity: they address a public who, when they respond, enrich art and writing with an infusion of new relations. This surface of mutual and multiple inscriptions emancipate the work from the fatalities that belong to personal destiny: an author's

---

1. Augé cites Leiris' riff on *modernité* that teases out the verb *merdoyer*: the word is a derivation of *merder*, to "screw up" or "go to shit," and contains *merde*, the French word for shit. By rearranging the letters of *modernité* to create *merdonité*, Leiris invents an amalgamation that assimilates the idea of waste into the modern.

work may survive him, and there is nothing metaphorical about that survival: any number of material signs may demonstrate it, at least for a while, and sometimes for a very long time.

To defend oneself against the idea of death means to be sure of living, meaning, for a human being, to be attuned to one's time and to other people, to be contemporary. This truth may be expressed in two ways: one must be completely of one's time to survive it; only someone who embodies his era can break free from it. Sartre made the point that at the heart of the particular, the universal makes itself known.

If one cannot be immortal, one can at least be sure of having existed and, then, not having been consciously or unconsciously anachronistic, out-of-date, out of life.

As for Olympia, she expresses and, literally, displays a spontaneous modernism. The ribbon at Olympia's throat is a sign of modernity. Olympia is "a perfectly contemporary young woman," "one of those women about whom you dream at night because you crossed her path that day." And yet, she is a "girl of her time," as is underlined by certain accessories and particularly the "thin black ribbon at her neck."

As for the painter or writer, it is a question of simultaneously observing the self and the era, of being "modern" in that sense. What the figure of Manet's Olympia ("a woman resting on a bed") reminds us, with her secular accessories, is that History exists, a "parade of fleeting episodes" that unfold simultaneously with the episodes of her life. The presence of the urbanite Olympia, through her modernity ("intensity, proximity, immediacy"), poses a challenge to anyone who contemplates her, particularly Leiris, who wonders how to situate her transience in relation to that of the era. To no longer belong to one's time is to no longer be a part of life, "is to be already a part of death." Hence the task he assigns himself: at least to grasp that "modern" that could very well escape his attention, extract from civilization the trait that defines the era.

Modernity? Every era has its characteristic traits, but some prolong or surpass it. Modernity, eternity; modernity is "the extreme point of an era," sustaining the alarming sensation of existing somewhere other than in the temporal.

In the background, Leiris's pen sketches out some quick considerations on the ambiguities of progress. But that is undoubtedly not his main subject. Fascism and racism in their diverse forms have yet to breathe their last breath; this fact is even more true now than it was thirty years ago. No doubt we have seen many modernities. The mass media show us the horrors of our world and invite us to consider that today's modernity, "an affront to its very name," has ceased to be modern. *Modernité, merdonité?*

Leiris has won his modest wager, and asserts his modernity through the subtle attention he simultaneously pays to the movements of his era and his own evolution — to the inescapable character of the singular fate whose form he observes coming to an end in a world of total and unpredictable evolution. A beautiful example of this belated modernity: Leiris, doubting what separates failure from success in literature, "grabs hold of the ribbon at Olympia's throat" like a rope that saves him from drowning. He thus confronts the final stage of life ("the past in ruins, the present in disarray, the future in tatters") by vigorously restating the question of a lifetime—*Who am I?*—while enabling us to hear in it the equivalent of *Who are we?*

I remember the day when Jean Jamin invited me to meet Michel Leiris for a genial, wine-soaked meal, during which he spoke to us about his relationship to literature, notably insisting with as much good humor as modesty on what, he claimed, he hadn't been able to accomplish. He said goodbye to us on the sidewalk. We watched him walk away towards Boulevard Raspail, a fragile and tenacious silhouette, and I hadn't the slightest doubt of having met not only a great writer, but a great witness of our time.

◇

All of a sudden, the bed lurches to the right and I find myself thrown to that side, so fast that I very nearly gasp for breath. The floor drops out from under me and when, more awake, I recover by rolling onto my back, although I had been sleeping on my right side, the ceiling then takes its turn at lurching towards the left. My eyes struggle to regain equilibrium and the ceiling spins several times before I manage to set myself right, a little like the way, after a switch in the tracks, a conductor corrects his steering after missing the rail on the first try.

Neither drunk on liquor or other intoxicant nor the victim of an earthquake, I have just had what is known as a dizzy spell, a malaise whose physiological mechanism (variable depending on the case, obviously) is as unknown to most people as it is to me. Given the even darker turn that my thoughts have taken since my recent birthday—one of those funereal milestones that some like to see turned into celebrations—this is cause for concern. And yet, I soon draw an optimistic conclusion from this minor warning sign: that fatal strait that I dread crossing to such an extreme, that seems approachable only after passing through a dense thicket that wounds me with its thorns, perhaps I could cross it in the blink of an eye, feeling only a rush of vertigo that, my clock having run out for good, won't even have time enough to clear.

◇

—*Listen, dear reader (for by reading me, you will become dear to me), and know that if I say anything here, it is more to speak than to say something.*

—*What? You're talking but not saying anything?*

—*In a manner of speaking. It's a figure of speech when I say that I'm speaking in order to speak: when I speak, it's certainly to say something, but (speaking frankly) I don't know what.*

—*You don't say. . . So, you don't know what you're talking about?*

—*Perhaps. . . But listen, who do you think you're talking to? I'm not some kid you can scold by claiming he doesn't know what he's saying. If I knew, I wouldn't have to say it. And as I've already said, I speak in order to speak and it's by saying it that I will know what I have to say.*

—*I always say. . . When you say white, when you say black, when you say yes, when you say no, when you say everything that comes into your head, what does that mean? What do you want to say?*

—*I want to say. And, that said, I'll say everything that speaks to me. Even if I shout it from the rooftops, there'll be nothing you can say about it.*

—*It goes without saying, but to put it bluntly, you sound like an awful bigmouth.*

—Say what you will, I'm not that loose-lipped: strictly speaking, I only speak (and I'll say no more) to quiet those things that leave us speechless, that prove that one day nothing will say anything to us anymore. Let that be said!

—My word, you talk like a book. . . No pun intended, but what more is there to say?

—You're telling me! And to think that you took me for a phrase-turner. . .

Bonjour,	Hello,
bonne année,	Happy new year,
bonne chance,	Good luck,
bon courage,	Hang in there,
bon appétit,	Enjoy your meal,
bonne route!	Happy trails!

May words return to those who are stifled by silence!

May ink draw vibrant arabesques on your white paper shroud!

May a spider spin a web in you, catching flies at your mercy!

May the table where your notebook lies open be a skiff with the wind in its sails!

May, when you take your seat, your chair and its quadrangle of feet not serve as the pillory's platform, but align with the cardinal points!

May the lamp that illuminates you teach you not to be a greedy flame!

May the pillow, your companion in sleep, be a satchel full of dreams!

May the ground you tread upon, hard or soft, assure you that you haven't gone mad!

May the houses on the street be, in your eyes, more windows than walls!

May your handful of remaining years, months, or days be embers, not dregs!

May the noose that strangles you unravel before time runs out!

May you embrace, in spirit, the companion your attrition keeps you from embracing in body!

May you be a purveyor of words and not their bumbling customer!

May your winter carnival, all damask and crystal, shimmer without eclipse!

◇

Many years ago—if my memory can still be taken at its word—a number of horse races, pretexts for wagers large and small but for which the institution of the trifecta was never established, were created under the guise of improving the equine race. This was, in fact, the proclaimed goal of at least one of the specialized societies, some of which presided over the organization of "flat" racecourses, steeple-chases, and hurdles (events for which Longchamp and Auteuil are still the hot spots in the Paris region), and the others—or a single other—over courses for harnessed or mounted trotting, which are more plebian events.

Do I inflict an infringement of the same order upon the truth when I assign to my activity of straddling the fountain pen, one I am loathe to practice as a game played merely for its own sake, this remotely humanitarian virtue: bringing subjects to light that others know nothing about, helping them to grasp matters in all of their depth, seeing things more clearly and broadly, knowing oneself better, improving oneself?

Unable to tattoo everything he had in his head over the surface of his skin, he decided—too obsessed with totality to accept leaving untouched those parts of his body that his hand could not easily reach—to confide to paper, rather than to the thin envelope lacked only by the écorché, what he wanted to make known about himself. But despite certain advantages (dodging the delicate problem of pagination, making use of a less limited space, making public those things that propriety would otherwise obligate him to keep private, making the medium of his message something more durable than his own body), it was only a last resort: with that vicarious approach—projecting himself onto a screen, rather than putting his body on the line by covering himself from head to toe with inscriptions and images bound to his physical mass even more intimately than the way an efflorescence of moss or lichen seems to cling to a rock—his discourse would never be as eloquent as his flesh, his life organ and receptacle of feeling, would have been if, making himself the object of a sort of inlay, he had superimposed on that natural grimoire, his human organism, a second grimoire full to bursting with signs that admitted no dead space.

At the Musée de l'Homme, the Magdalenian III-era engraving in stone representing a woman (obese, we think) whose fringed garment seems to have been reproduced with great accuracy.

In Crete—where I have never been—the fresco, so contemporary despite its antiquity, named "The Parisians."

In Sicily, the women in bikinis appearing in a Roman mosaic in the Piazza Armerina.

At the Accademia in Venice, in the background of one of Carpaccio's paintings depicting scenes from the life of Saint Ursula—specifically, the arrival of English ambassadors in Brittany—the dogs walking around a square full of people whom the artist unquestionably wanted dressed in the latest fashions of the day, from the young dandies up to (what appears to be) a dwarf as fat as a Buddha; then—in The Dream of St. Ursula, a later episode—the fine pair of slippers neatly arranged at the foot of the bed of the sleeping saint.

Turner's famous painting (Rain, Steam, and Speed in the National Gallery) depicting the blackness of a locomotive amidst a luminous brew of color, hence contrasting with and emerging from chaos.

The ribbon tied around the neck of Manet's Olympia and the mules that her feet, as explicitly naked as her entire body appears to be as a result of the addition of those accessories, seem ready to lose.

The watch-bracelets that, encircling their wrists, prevent many of the innumerable nudes whom Picasso sketched or painted from becoming mythological Venuses.

The hypodermic needle that Bacon planted in the arm of a female nude that, by modernizing her, renders the figure more authentically present.

The pretty little slipper that reveals Perrault's Cinderella, the Cinderella of Christmas pantomime plays, and—when transformed into a bracelet—Rossini's Cenerentola.

In the theatre, the powdered skull, the walking statue, the razor, the fool's marotte, the white uniform, the severed head on a platter, etc., that conjure up ghosts for Hamlet, Don Juan, Figaro, Rigoletto, l'Aiglon, Salomé and others.

The stocking that the girl of yesteryear kept on to prevent herself from dissolving into the edenic blur of total nudity.

The detail we touch with our fingers, bait we sink our teeth into, that makes Saint Thomases of us.

Expected or unexpected, the moment that exposes and disarms the sinister passage of time.

$\diamond$

My father gave me
Rubies, rubettes,
My father gave me
Ribbons of satin. . .

Refrain that returns to me from childhood, sung quietly by a woman or a little girl. On the way, it has become coated with a melancholic sheen.

In Paris, 1959, in the expressly cultural setting of the Théatre de Nations, which produced a variety of performances every year that eventually came from very far away and were sometimes extremely beautiful, the Frankfurt Opera presented, under the musical direction of Georg Solti, *The Marriage of Figaro*. A connoisseur who was even the slightest bit particular would have been put off by the fact that this work by Mozart and da Ponte was sung in German and not Italian, but this didn't prevent me, more gourmand than gourmet in many respects, from being enraptured by the evening.

At the end of the "Air militaire" with which the first act draws to a close (that famous air that Mozart recovers as a quotation in one of *Don Juan*'s final scenes, as if to infuse the sacrilegious feast with a bit of mischief and perhaps, on a deeper level, as if this anachronistic reminder, an irruption of the now within a legendary tragedy, indicates that we are already living outside of time at the moment when, with the walking statue, the supernatural makes its radiant entrance) we witness Chérubin—a graceful cantatrice, as vocally effortless as she is convincing in her spirited performance of a libertine in training —throw from the back of the stage, and with enough force that the projectile passes above the heads of the musicians assembled in their pit, the hat (in this instance a tricorne) that is no longer suitable now that, in order that he be sent away, Chérubin has been elevated from the rank of page to officer. With his left hand, the maestro Solti catches the object in flight, while he continues to conduct with his right hand holding the baton for the several remaining measures.

Apparently improvised, this gag had two virtues at the very least: in a single gesture, it eliminated any and all of the distance that is almost always too rigidly divided in our theaters between set and orchestra, as well as between stage and audience, and its casualness demonstrated an easygoing intimacy with the masterpiece that is all too frequently performed with a seriousness that borders on pedantry. An impulsive conclusion of a brilliant performance, it seemed to respond spontaneously to the idea that if you wish to do something extraordinary, you must leave a bit of space for the living and unforeseen reality of the *happening**,[1] even in a performance whose progression is very classically regulated.

Nevertheless, I must say that before it inspired this theoretical reflection concerning the art of performance, the prank charmed me and made me immediately think (the action's implied location no doubt helped in this) of the brazen authority that, if it comes at the proper moment, may be produced by what the language of bullfighting calls an *adorno*, and in which, without any ham-handed showing off, the toreador inserts an addendum into a magisterial labor with no other goal than to demonstrate the extent to which he dominates the animal he is fighting.

But perhaps this is a fortuitous analogy, resting on another marginal detail that made me skid off from opera's prestiges to those of the bullring. Chérubin's gesture, creating a bridge

---

1. Translator's Note: words that appear in English in the original text have been marked with an asterisk.

between fiction and reality by making his tricorne soar above the orchestra and its rows of music stands, actually reminded me, if not in spirit at least in form, of the matador's gesture of throwing the *montera* that he had been wearing to the man or woman to whom, on the other side of the circular corridor where minions such as matadors' assistants sit, he dedicates the toro he is readying himself to kill.

◇

In front of Regan, whom we will soon see voluptuously snaking her gorgeous arms, the Duke of Cornwall gouges out the eye of the elderly Count of Gloucester, tied to the stake. A sudden blackout, both on stage and in the hall, and for a moment it is pitch dark. Same trick for the second eye, and again the spectator has the cruel, abrupt sensation of having suddenly become blind himself.

In this way, the paroxysmal form of theater described by Antonin Artaud unexpectedly took shape in an English production of *King Lear*, whose staging was flatly historical and entirely banal from beginning to end.

◇

By the bed where Desdemona has just been put to death by her husband—in whom Iago planted the idea that the young noblewoman who had scandalously run off with him, a man of another class and another race, was bound to betray him sooner or later—a high-backed chair. Very tall and very strong, the tenor playing Othello that night at the Paris Opera (I could give you the precise date, but to do so I would have to scavenge through the messy cabinet holding my personal archives in order to find the program that I kept, as I do for almost all of the performances I attend unless they were only mildly interesting, work which would hardly be proportionate to the minor importance of that chronological detail), the Wagnerian tenor Hans Beirer, whom I had already heard and appreciated in other roles, presses his two hands on the back of the chair. The chair collapses under his weight and, for a moment, Othello seems about to fall. But the singer corrects himself and the incident that, if a fall had occurred, would have unexpectedly thrown the drama into the tall grass of the burlesque proves, on the contrary, to be a happy accident. No calculated stage direction could have illustrated the Moor's Herculean strength and his bewildered state in a more convincing way.

◇

Achilles, wearing a woman's dress, now wails before Patrocles' outstretched corpse, nearly naked and bleeding at his feet. He neither recites nor, suffice it to say, acts, but as he stands facing the audience he howls, moans, lows, brays, and trumpets, and this outburst pierces a hole in the heart of the tragedy. With his bestial cry, the actor suddenly makes himself so present—separated from us by as few screens as he is from his character—that it's almost disturbing. Is it not reality itself that obscenely erupts, in all its terrible rawness? No longer Alan Howard, playing one of the main roles in *Troilus and Cressida*, but Achilles himself, the wrecked and furious lover who with his delirious clamor punctures the poetic fabric of which the Trojan War is the thread and, leaving the cloud of the legend behind, appears right in front of us to give voice to our unfathomable wound.

In the second act of *The Tragedy of King Christophe*, the play in which Aimé Césaire made a hero of Shakespearean proportions out of a former slave who became king, one character makes an appearance in only one short scene: after being sent by Louis XVIII to invite Christophe, who reigns over the north of Haiti, to return to the heart of France, the Spanish Franco de Medina provokes the anger of the monarch, who then condemns him to death. We see him walk towards the execution site, escorted by several soldiers. The role is limited to an entrance, a couple of brief ripostes, and an exit—a shallow role, and entirely incidental, a "nothing" part that is difficult to imagine any actor making memorable. And nothing is what, until this production (one of the ones that were staged in Dakar in 1965), those who were responsible for it ever made of it, however hard they may have tried!

But, as luck would have it, Jean-Marie Serreau, the producer and director of the troupe, was forced to play the role at the last minute to replace the incumbent at the time, who had been called to Paris on some kind of business. Neither Césaire nor any of his friends who like myself were in the audience were aware of this replacement. Great, then, was our surprise when this new Franco of Medina appeared onstage and we saw this paltry character suddenly become something more than the bland silhouette to which we were accustomed.

Two ideas as simple as ABC. Historically, Franco de Medina was a Spaniard and so it goes without saying that his French pronunciation suffered for it—a chance for Serreau to give the character some caricaturish vigor by endowing him with a thick accent. Theatrically, his exit posed a problem: how should he walk away to die? An afflicted pace would have been too melodramatic and a martial one too "patriotic," so the role's interpreters had until then prudently abstained from any psychological indication, which brought the scene to an abrupt end. But Serreau knew how to handle the situation by adding a visible limp to the burlesque accent of his Franco de Medina, a double blow since, on the one hand, he individualized it even more by making the character lame and, on the other, conferred upon Franco an immediate theatrical interest by having him walk to his death while pitifully dragging his leg, perhaps as gouty as his royal patron.

I've always admired that an actor was able, through his ingenuity, to give substance to a role that Césaire had only introduced into his play to emphasize one side of Christophe's character. Serreau took hold of the various givens and resolved the problem with brio: a man of the theatre who yielded to the exigencies of the performance but remained scrupulous enough to satisfy them without becoming gratuitous. Thus fantasy, united with authenticity, led to the absolute *presence* of a figure who formerly did not exist.

◇

The nail clipping, lock of hair or other fragment of a body through which magic may be practiced.

In the work of Sigmund Freud, whom a French intellectual in the '20s compared to a detective (namely, Nick Carter) whose mystery pursuits were based on infinitesimal clues, the slight thing—slip, memory lapse. . .—filled with great significance.

In the work of Marcel Proust, who spent practically all of his time trying to neutralize time, the fugitive sensation that causes a broad swath of memory to resurface.

Newton's apple, the precise and concrete case from which one begins to elaborate a theory.

On the contrary, the drop of water that makes the vessel overflow.

◇

As opposed to my mother's cousin, who thought the painting was a masterpiece, my father was essentially of the opinion that Manet's *Olympia* was a lifeless figure whose formal stiffness was as repellent as her almost cadaverous complexion. A painter in his spare time who signed the articles he published in private associations or parishes' obscure bulletins "Louis de Lutèce"— Louis like Louis XIV, but born in Paris like Villon—this modest civil servant, who fancied himself an art critic and whose irreverent glibness was a flower in his slightly bohemian although fundamentally narrow-minded and bourgeois lapel, represented the modernist of the family as far as the fine arts were concerned.

It was very early on (probably shortly after the transfer from Luxembourg to the Louvre that marked her definitive consecration and when I was a very young boy, more familiar with the Church of Notre-Dame-d'Auteuil than those secular temples that are museums) that I got wind of *Olympia*, and so the first time that I saw her, either in flesh and blood, if I may say so, or under the meager auspices of a photographic reproduction, she wasn't completely unknown to me. Isn't it because of the echoes of the disagreement she caused so long ago between my father, the philistine, and his relative by marriage, the refined connoisseur, that to me she remains clad in the singular charm of the famous but often misunderstood work that, passionately contested and regarded by some as a sin against good taste, is imbued—despite so much incense— with a slight whiff of heresy?

It was my turn, due to aging, to suffer the consequences of the operation from which my father, after enduring terrible agonies, had died. Even though it was understood that, because of surgical advances, it was no longer the grave affair it once had been, I was still very much afraid. Less, certainly, because a dramatic death seemed possible than because of the suffering that, to my mind, such an intervention would inevitably cause. Despite all of the reassuring things I was told—"You'll suffer for an hour at the most," one person assured me, without realizing that to me even an hour seemed too long—I felt destined for unbearable moments and, what's more, even the idea of a wound to the most private part of my body and the very special care that my state would require left me absolutely horrified. That is why, as soon as I had decided not to wait to resort to a radical treatment that would put an end to the troubles whose best case scenario was that they would not intensify too quickly, I found myself face to face with my fear, and couldn't help but be profoundly disturbed by it. Not only did I think about it during the day, but panic assaulted me at least once in the dead of night, in a fanciful form.

No images came, but a sort of purely abstract meditation—or speculation—on what awaited me. In my patently ethnological mind, the thing presented itself in an absurd way, as a fact of cultural contact: just as one group of people might borrow certain cultural traits from another group to whom they find themselves related, I would soon require certain habits that were brand new to me, and if I were to mentally prepare myself, I would be entirely ready to take that plunge into another civilization: my entrance into the clinic. I was informed, without really knowing which came first, that the operation had two distinct phases: one, technical, was the *procedure* [*procédé*], which notably required that after anesthesia I would regain consciousness with a catheter in my penis; the other, psychological, was *adoption* or *adaptation*. There was nothing harrowing about that and I felt, on the contrary, that all of this, far from asking the impossible, was essentially a question of good faith. While reflecting upon it several days afterwards, I realized that in my nocturnal flight of fancy whose details I was still struggling to grasp, it was a matter of, in sum, taking the catheter just as one civilization takes a bow or a weaving loom from another and, continuing this technological train of thought, I asked myself if the term "procedure," which alluded to the fact that I would have to adopt the habit of wearing a catheter until my recovery, couldn't apply to the object itself while adapting to this temporary infirmity, just as the word "pratique" is used, outside of its primary meaning, to designate the little tinplate implement that puppeteers use to make their voices shrill. An apparently satisfactory explanation, one to which I would have kept if another, much simpler one had not also presented itself. Three lines read in a dictionary by chance, during a search regarding a very different matter, had in fact reminded me that the word "procedure" also materializes in an object: the leather round affixed to the end of a billiard cue, a so-called *queue à procédé*, (in this case, a barely allusive description of my virility such as it would be for some time).

To transform the dreaded event into a phenomenon analogous to some of those I had studied professionally was one method of minimizing it. If it weren't, would I have ever thought of the bow, the weaving loom and the piece of tin metal, totally aberrant substitutes for the thin *foreign body* whose presence I would be forced to admit?

Once that threshold had been crossed, I discovered that I had in fact been quite wrong to consider something tragic that, when all was said and done, proved to be more on the level of a enema bag in an old slapstick routine than a sword or a dagger. There was no heroism to display, only managing a farce that was more distasteful than it was atrocious, and the need to re-educate myself in one of the body's lowest functions, after having removed the engine that had allowed for it, simply made me depressed—apart from an unexpected but all the more challenging episode when, after I had finished convalescing and thought the matter was behind me, I had, because of a benign complication that required attention, to subject myself to yet another examination that caused me even more pain than the worst of what I had previously endured (the paradoxical discomfort of the first night, a burning sensation of unsatisfied need while in truth I could eliminate without obstacle). A practical joke that threw me into the pit of the absurd—like the sugar cube that floats instead of melts or the cigarette that explodes after several puffs—was what the ordeal seemed to be in the end, after misunderstanding and anticipation had made me dissemble so deeply in order to strengthen my courage. . .

"Look, you're a man again!" announced my nurse, a young, cheerful, and polite pied-noir originally from Sidi-bel-Abbès, when she liberated me from the unwelcome pipe. But which man? The question remains, and even if it were complete, my medical *curriculm vitae* would provide only a lacunary response.

◇

The word "love," a red flag.
The word "adieu," a folded handkerchief.

I thought of this incident, hardly worthy of such a name, for the first time—and that was already once too many—when I made it the subject of a note written in cursive, dated 14 November 1975, in the journal that I've kept only sporadically for some time now but in which I still occasionally record some fact that struck me for some reason or other or some idea that came to me and that, perhaps wrongly, I don't want to let slip away. And as I began writing this entry, I almost immediately fell prey to a sort of fascination that made me want to relate in as much detail as possible, without falling into inaccuracy or even invention, a story that was hardly worth writing down, even in very few words: a speck of dust amidst the innumerable specks of dust that memory ordinarily doesn't want to be bothered with, and wouldn't have room for if it did. Half in an honest desire for exhaustiveness, half for the satisfaction found in substituting a verbal ceremony for the ridiculous affair that had been made available to me but hadn't taken place and that drew from its incompletion (as well as from the fact that, even if had I wholeheartedly wanted it to succeed, my organic deterioration would have prohibited its consummation) its power to obsess, I wrote this sort of récit with more attention than was necessary and with care that was disproportionate to the triviality of its pretext.

On the uneven pavement of the rue des Capucines, which onomastics dedicate either to the nasturtium or the nun, one Friday, the day that falls under Venus' aegis. Just before the boulevard, a stylish sports car (a Sunbeam or Triumph), very low to the ground and the color of a buttercup, pulls up beside me. Two young, thin women, fairly well-dressed, occupy the front seats. The one on the left is a brunette with long hair and a rather serious expression; the one on the right, dressed more brightly than her neighbor, who's wearing a black or other somber-colored coat on top of a white blouse (which suits her complexion), has shorter blond or chestnut hair and resembles—enough to bring me to the brink of disgust—a young American girl I know, the daughter of an excellent family who works for the Museum of Modern Art and whose impish face and svelte silhouette are most seductive.

A dialogue begins between these two characters and myself, who mistakes them at first for two tourists looking for directions.

The Blonde (who catches my attention first from the passenger seat, the girl next to her looking like the confidante in classical theatre): Wanna go for a drive?

Me (placing my two hands on the door with the window down): Where?

The Blonde (and probably the Brunette, in chorus): Not far. . .

A pause, then in a soft voice and with a charming smile:

The Blonde: We could make love. . .

Me (friendly and polite): That's very kind of you. But I'm a little old.

The Blonde (aloof, but still smooth): Ok, fine!

The car immediately pulls away, and I see it stop again at a red light several meters away, this time towards the middle of the street.

Continuing on my way—on the rue de Sèze, on the right side of the street heading towards the rue Chauveau-Lagarde, a street I know well because I frequent one of its shops, a dog kennel on the corner of the boulevard Malesherbes—I have a second encounter: a woman who is clearly drunk and wrapped in a thick fur coat (real or fake leopard, I'm not sure which), entirely lacking in grace despite her attention to style, is walking towards me. At the exact moment she passes me, she gives me—brusquely rolling up her lips that suddenly form an upside-down circumflex accent—a red smile that vanishes just as quickly as it appears, since nothing in my attitude indicates that I had considered her silent offer for even a second. About her, perhaps because of her age, I will have no regrets, whereas the image of the two sirens, whose breasts I hadn't even seen in their full glory and whom I left to drown in the oceanic clamor of the shores of Madeleine and l'Opera, will continue to haunt me. Their search will, I am sure, soon prove fruitful and I hope that all of the money and perhaps the pleasure that they seek will come to them in spades. But, while I think of the other woman's silhouette (the one with the too-mechanical and too-heavily painted mouth) as the ghostly appearance of an elderly *kabuki* actor miming the affectations of a courtesan to stylized excess, the fresh image of the two girls who offered to drive me towards who knows what bedroom or banal studio that would for a time become an eden as long as I was up to the rapture, takes the form of a bitter and tender memory that I trust will be long in disappearing.

A memory that, in truth, would have quickly ceased to torment me if, instead of being dictated by the fear of a yes that would have certainly led me to humiliate myself, the no with which I had refused the invitation of the two beautiful women had been a choice I made on my own free will (a choice that, little inclined to adulterous escapades, I would have steered towards the negative, having no taste for venal affairs and, what's more, lacking spare time on that particular day).

And yet, since this dubious reverie persists like a tenacious fever, I can't help but wonder if, had I endured the ordeal without disaster, I would have picked up the habit, tawdry yet beneficial, of rekindling a cherished part of my life (one I have difficulty accepting has permanently faded) on the sly from time to time with good-natured sorceresses with a few tricks up their sleeves?

But, on the other hand, had the experience ended in the failure I dreaded, it might have become something worse than humiliating: renowned for resuscitating the dead as much as for corrupting saints, and annoyed by the inertia of their sad cavalier, cheated (as generous as I might have been) of their ambition to sell themselves to geriatrics, the two nymphs—or if I hadn't been invited to a threesome, my favorite, the blonde—might have turned into harpies and drowned me in contempt, foul insults, even, right at the moment when, instead of plunging the knife into my heart, they should have been licking my wounds. Hence the promised delights might have turned into torture, and the idyll an explosion of mutual resentment.

Even so, after my fanatic obsession had weakened enough for it to yield to critical reflection (after avatars such as the idea that one elegant solution would have been to inform my two accomplices, if I had had two, that I only wanted to be a titillated witness to their gambols), I think—source of another kind of melancholy—that I must really be in a terribly neurotic state for something so minor, politely rebuffing the mercantile advances of two attractive girls by confessing I'm an old man, to trouble me so much.

The word "pleasure," an empty shell.
The word "courage," a scrubbing brush.

◇

—"What do you think you're looking at? You go to hell!"

That's what—right when we crossed each other in the rue Dauphine, whose series of ground-floor shops include my pharmacy, my tobacconist, and the unassuming hair salon where a sweet young woman trims my hair every week with clippers and scissors—the relatively young but pale and mangled character yelled as he staggered, several meters in front of me, in the middle of a side street. I had barely laid eyes on him, although with a repugnance that he might have assumed (conscious no doubt of his state and the disapproval that might result from it) but certainly didn't have time to notice, as I had only given him the slightest glance.

—"Me too!" I declared without turning around, making the kind of gesture with my right hand hanging by my side that you make while trying to calm down a yippy little dog when he snaps at you.

—"You can go to hell two times!" was the *fortissimo* response of my howler monkey, while I continued on my way with the priggish dignity of a man immune to slander issuing from someone so far beneath him, someone whose head is spinning either from temporary drunkenness or a permanent condition, which led me to believe the *minus habens* look (disheveled, but more petit-bourgeois than vagrant) that had struck me in this stranger who quickly became my detractor.

Nobly, I kept walking with the same measured pace I had used before the altercation. Nobly, but gripped internally by a frisson of fear. Fear of what? Certainly not of the violent offenses this malingerer could, if anger drove him to it, have committed against me (I'm no athlete, but I'm certain that this wretch would at the most have dragged me into a grotesque fight that caused no serious damage either to him or to me). Fear, truthfully, like the fear of a ghost, represented here by a living being who seemed like nothing but trash. Fear, as if the spectacle of a human being reduced to a derelict reminds you that you too are destined to deteriorate when, physically, you are at the end of your rope and as if, age having destroyed my defenses at the very moment when I need them more than ever before, my abstract fear of the inevitable were now deep enough that almost anything could awaken it and that it manifests, practically, as a fear of everything.

The horror, too, of being an object of hatred, and the disgust of belonging to a universe in which the existence of certain miseries that no reasonable palliative can remedy is enough to expose its fundamental cruelty.

At the Place de Furstenberg, adorned by a lamppost whose five globes look like large white grapes in the trellis formed by the branches of the four trees planted around it, a man between two centuries, rather thin and ravaged, appears to be walking back from the rue Jacob. Heading towards the south side of the square (near the Rue de L'Abbaye, where the district's police commissioner is located), he stops at a rather squalid ground-floor window, on his left just as it is on mine, and—like a guy who knows all the good spots—places the half-full bottle he holds in his hand on the window frame. Then he quietly walks away, as if he were in his own home and as if he were prudently treating the stone ledge of the barred window like a cellar where he stowed away the wine he still had to drink.

I take the Rue de l'Abbaye towards Saint-Germain-de-Prês, where I am supposed to meet—at Deux-Magots, which will turn out to be closed for the season—two American friends, one of whom I haven't seen in a long time and who had telephoned to say that she was passing through Paris and had some free time that night. After a brief stop at Le Mabillon, a café at the crossroads of rue de Buci and the rue de l'Échaudé, where we had just enough time (since their schedule was very tight) to chat a bit while the two of them drank a kir and I had a coffee, once my two friends had left, I crossed the Place de Furstenberg a second time, walking then towards Rue Jacob on my way back home after going to the underground parking lot at Saint-Germain-des-Prés where my friend's friend had left her car after not being able to find another spot. Almost immediately I notice the man from earlier on, who this time again seems to be coming from the Rue Jacob. Wanting, no doubt, to take at least a couple of swigs from the bottle that he had carefully placed on that windowsill (like provisions in a pantry or communion wine on an altar table), he returns, I suppose, to this semblance of an open-air bistro he created as if he were a toreador returning to his *querencia* in the middle of a bullfight. His appearance hasn't changed, and he advances in my direction with the same slight stagger as before. But—and this is something new, unless I hadn't seen it an hour ago when our respective positions were different—the left side of his face, which is for me the right side, is now half-covered by a large and ugly reddish bruise that marks his forehead, one side of his nose, and half of one cheek.

Did he fall down? Did he crash into something? Was he beaten?

To know for sure, I would have had to question him. But I am wary of making contact with unknown drunks who might be loose cannons, and anyway I hadn't the slightest right to interfere in his private affairs, as much as his metamorphosis (or what seemed like one to me) had aroused my curiosity.

As *Olympia* or *Mlle V. en costume d'espada*, Victorine Meurent, Édouard Manet's model, may be painted lying down or standing up, undressed or clad in elegant, black culottes that try—without success—to masculinize her form, but everything about her signifies Beauty. And nothing waters down that Beauty by removing it from its conditions and placing it in the heights of the sublime. In the bedroom or in full sun, stretched out on a bed or with her feet firmly planted on the sand of a bullring, receiving a bouquet without giving it the slightest attention or raising her épée as if sagaciously conducting a tragic symphony (while in her left hand the flourishing cape is almost the same shade of pink as the large bow tucked behind the ear of the impassive Olympia), she remains someone whose pretty, slightly heavy face belongs, despite the passing of more than a century, to a perfectly contemporary young woman and who, most worldly, could very well be one of those creatures about whom you dream at night because you crossed her path that day.

Awkwardly executed in black and colored pencil, the drawing—which used up the entire surface of a piece of foolscap paper—presented a series of scenes, each more bloody than the last, that told either of a single accident shown with its direct effects, or several different accidents; I no longer remember if they were simultaneous (with nothing connecting them except for coincidence) or if, in a kind of catastrophic chain reaction, they were set off by each other. The principal episode was the derailment of a streetcar or its collision with another vehicle. Blood spurted everywhere, and even the birds in the sky, after being splashed or becoming victims of some calamity accorded to the ambient disaster, were dripping with it.

A taste for the color red—the most dazzling color of all—probably began for many with the choice of a similar subject, while conversely, a good part of red's power of attraction on the passionate doodler that I was during a good part of my childhood was due (make no mistake) to the fact of its being, par excellence, the color of tragedy, for any real tragedy must involve the gushing of blood.

◇

In the dingy, furnished hotel room, on the floor over which the empty bottle had rolled and where the greatest disorder reigned (the table overturned, the laundry scattered, the dishes smashed), a man in large, probably hobnailed boots and whose unbuttoned shirt revealed his hairy chest was sitting on a chair. In a daze, he looked neither at the upside-down crib nor the bundle (of dirty linen, one might have said) that now was the baby whose skull he had shattered by throwing it against the wall. The wife was not there, either because the maniac had chased her away with punches and kicks before or after the tragedy, or because she had left—too late—to fetch the landlords (or in their absence, the police, perhaps playing cards for drinks nearby) to deal with the companion who this time had gone too far. As soon as day broke, a large, clotted stain that was not a vomit stain was clearly visible, starring the flowered wallpaper that had faded with time and increasing gloom. What had the fight been about: was the soup not hot enough for him (who very quickly had *seen red*), or for her (whining, like always), was it his drunken return?

When I left her after I ran into her, not really by accident since it wasn't unusual that we would both be there that afternoon, I kissed both cheeks of my Queen of Spades, always smiling despite her elegant, somber look of a bird of prey.

When they touched them, my lips were once again startled by the infantile roundness of her cheeks, just as my eyes, while they saw nothing new there, were surprised by her height, which her high heels (effortlessly) raised slightly above my own.

That I took leave of her so affectionately proves that I remain attached to the time when, exhilarated by the trip to the country that had reunited us and rekindled all my dreams, I became what in another era would have been called her faithful servant. But if that gesture accompanying the "au revoir" I gave her proved she need only reappear for her ambiguous charm to begin to dominate me again—albeit only when she is there—within reach—and not an hour more—it reflected no serious desire to replay a card I had lost on years ago.

A card that in truth I hadn't really played, except in a game akin to a waking dream, for I was committed elsewhere and knew all along that when luck, familiar with misdealing, made it—a mirage—fall into my hands, it was already too late.

◇

Grace, Nonchalance, Frivolity could be the motto of that Paris article, Olympia. With no other role than to place her body center stage and signify its glory, her sparse additions of jewelry that hide nothing and the gallantly sent bouquet beside her define her as someone whose high price, uniquely justified by the joys this head-turner seems to promise, is beyond all rational measure. It matters little that the image realized by Édouard Manet is of the order of things that are subject to fluctuations in market value; we don't know how to measure this explicitly seductive figure, fashioned by sorcerer's hands and from which, in a work that seems to have been painted solely for the artist's pleasure or to fantasize about the luxurious creature that work evokes, utilitarian utility is cynically absent in broad strokes or fine detail.

◇

My lover,
my friend,
my mascot,
my totem,
my talisman,
my godsend,
my fairy pond,
my balm,
my mother,
my murmur,
my music,
my sweet,
my sight,
my lookout,
my shore,
my ruby,
my ribbon,
my rebel,
my light,
my ray of sun,
my bright spell,
my lifeboat,
my other half,
my only one,
my dearest,
my millenium!

◇

Between these two people who placed sexual difference between parentheses and who found themselves only more deeply connected, was there—a negative, but uniquely powerful relation—the complicity of a tacit prohibition that, applying only to them, would have ostracized them from the coterie (whose mores were hardly rigorous) to which they belonged? Or rather, was it he, under the pretense of deep friendship for that woman who like himself was anchored to someone else, who had underhandedly claimed her for himself—avoiding every obstacle—by making her without anyone knowing anything about it, even herself, his untouchable Dulcinea?

(Already in part a fiction, such is the blueprint of the novel that could be written by someone who, without puritanical fidelity to the transcription of facts, asks this question from under the cloak of a conventional *he*, if while developing his theme he could put details into play that, pertinent or gratuitous, real or imagined, and relative to no matter what—characters, incidents, times, places, etc.—not only describe the thing in the greatest detail, but infuse the entirety of the text thus punctuated by hot spots with a reality that speaks for itself.)

◇

Lace, braids, trimmings, ribbons, cords. . . Did Mme Sapin, whom I remember having met as a child without knowing what her relationship was (surely it was distant) to my father and mother, run a notions shop? Was she a lace-maker? Or did she practice some other trade? As far as I can remember, this woman, probably a widow, lived alone with her nephew whose physique (suggesting that his first name, Prosper, had encouraged him to prosper in an obscene way) was the kind you don't forget: obese, with the purple complexion of an apoplectic, hardly more refined in mind than he was in body but considered to be a good guy, already a man in my view at the time and about whom I won-der—with no less uncertainty than I have regarding the lady's former occupation—if he hadn't helped her, as an employee and perhaps eventually as a successor, to run her modest enterprise. But did this little shop actually exist? Or is it an imaged transla-tion, a type of hieroglyph that, in my mind's search for a positive revival, replaces the terms (too abstract, in my opinion) "old-fashioned," "mean-spirited," and "petit-bourgeois"?

My maternal uncle—who understood matters of the heart and was considered to be an expert on feminine beauty—was sometimes astonished that when she was younger, this thin, ugly, and reputedly nasty creature could have been so beauti-ful (he explained) in the gown she had worn to some wedding or celebration he had also attended, despite his customary unsociability.

And I swear that I am not embellishing when I recall that this Mme Sapin, so charming when she was still the "young Sapin" (as my uncle called her) but who became almost as unattractive as Carabosse the Wicked Fairy once she had grown old, as if she had been corroded by her own acidity, actually lived on the rue de l'Arbre-Sec [Dry Tree Street] at the time when I escorted my mother on a visit there that she made purely out of politeness.

I learned from my older sister—whose almost flawless memory surprises me as much as the cheerfulness she has held on to after more than 90 years—that the small shop whose exact nature I couldn't remember and whose existence I ended up doubting existed had been managed by the nephew following his aunt. What was sold there, the only article, or at least the principal article, was, my sister reminded me, nets that covered women's hair, which—more succinctly, and happy to use the proper term—I will call "snoods."

Another strand of the web: I also learned from my sister (who, according to the cold facts of genealogy, is actually a cousin who was introduced into our household after the premature death of her father, my father's brother) that she herself was related to the shopkeeper, and so could very directly sort out not only by birthright but familial status the tangle of ins and outs and whys and wherefores of this person whose charms, now completely worn away, were wryly extolled by my uncle, who claimed he would have crossed Paris on his knees to have her.

◇

In the completely unphantasmagorical and contemporary novel I would like to write—a pervasive desire that, needless to say, has produced neither the slightest embryo of a plan, nor even an idea for a scene to develop or, heady perfume, an ambience to create—naturally there would be men and women. But who would they be? Where would they be? What would they do?

If I care about inventing characters who would be something more than portraits in disguise (mine and those of the people I know) but would exist on their own and, acting independently of my decisions, take me completely by surprise—since if they are merely copies or talking puppets whose actions have nothing to teach me, what good is writing a novel?—I'm doomed from the start. First problem: what occupations do I give them? I can't make them workers or farmers: the worlds of factories and construction sites and the rural are so foreign to me that, even with painstaking research, I wouldn't be able to write about them in any convincing way. Equally impossible, if I want them to work at something instead of lording it over a quasi-abstract empyrean of idleness, to make the protagonist a writer, an artist or, in some way or another, what is commonly (and arbitrarily) understood as an "intellectual": to locate him as such would make him breathe an air too close to the one I breathe for me to hope to see him take flight on his own. It might be possible, of course, to assign him an industrial, commercial, or financial occupation, a so-called liberal profession, an administrative position at whatever level, or who knows what? But, fearing a bit absurdly that a social motive of this kind would deprive him of poetic dimension as much as a badly chosen first and last name would, I'm absolutely loath to do so. To assign him the status of a young man who has not yet found his place (but what position would he be shooting for?) would only displace the problem and besides, pursuing a character who is considered to be only a second-class citizen (an artisan or worker employed in a more or less marginal fashion) would, given how suspicious I am of most everything, risk sliding into cheap picturesque, just as it would be ill-advised to make him—an equally flimsy artifice—a sort of licensed migrant (a diplomat who's constantly traveling and perhaps at risk of being taken hostage, an airplane pilot or flight attendant, an itinerant representative of an international firm, a photojournalist, a teacher of bridge or some other amusement that would allow him to travel between luxurious residences and winter or summer homes, etc.) or rather, conversely, a sedentary person who communes with nature—a property owner, horticulturist, or meteorologist whose voice eventually becomes famous over the radio—such close ties that this fixation with the land or the prodigious theater of its sky blue envelope would open the door to the most traditional clichés. A man whose past was disrupted by revolution but who, disillusioned, now earns his living practicing a profession he has no interest in, after having lived for so long as a paid employee of the militant organization he was once so passionate about, a man now without any real foundation, and altogether equidistant between nomadism and rootedness, might be a good axis around which to make all of history spin. And yet, if I were to choose this kind of hero or anti-hero (a character who would be familiar enough for me to invent him and at the same time different enough so that

I wouldn't suffer too close a resemblance), it would be impossible not to orient my novel towards the political situation that, as the horizon looks bleaker than ever, is currently so hopeless. Why not then simply write an essay that might—who knows?—have some chance of being more useful than a fiction. . . Same problem for the element that is in my opinion essential, since a novel in which love plays no part would not provide me, despite its beauty and even if it does touch upon some question that seems fundamental, with a myth capable of quenching my thirst as fully as I would like: the heroine, who might not have any pro-fession at all, either honorable or dishonorable, but who needs at least some kind of specialized activity (a sport such as horseback riding in the open air or swimming in any spot that allows for it other than in swimming pools, reading, the leisure arts, music appreciation, flower arranging, dogs, cats, or what have you) and whom, in any case, it would make sense to define either according to her background, which may not necessarily be any more French than that of her partner, or from the company she keeps, unless we make her a recluse by choice, or secluded on account of some miserable condition that cuts her off from the world with, if a truly sordid mind prevails, a child whom she struggles to raise (unless it is her male counterpart who finds himself afflicted by these types of concerns).

Certainly, the prejudicial difficulties that I enumerate here—awkwardly, given the very weakness of my novelistic vein, and simplifying them besides, since in reality I would not be content with a couple who were surrounded by supporting characters or augmented by a third party whose role would directly or indi-rectly turn matters into a bedroom farce—could technically have been the obstacles that my desire to write a novel has been unable to overcome. And yet, I wonder if it isn't my egotism—my eter-nal inability to forget myself—that has always barred me from that domain: inventing characters who were vivid enough to break away from me, live their own lives, and substitute their lives for my own in some way has no doubt been beyond my power. Just as I have not had children, I will not have written a novel, a discourse more free and alert (such was my hope), closer to life as it unfolds on the outside and hence more aerated, conforming more to that state of pure inebriation of existence that I would like to achieve if such a conversion were possible for me, a discourse that is more relaxed and, in that alone, more likely than the ones I have for so long drawn from the vacuum of the exacting consideration of myself to allow me to reach that goal, as simple as ABC but just out of my reach. Neither human figures projected onto paper, nor children cast out in the thick of the world. . . I have a great fear that the most decisive cause of this double infertility that could largely be explained in terms of a well-reasoned refusal—not giving birth in order not to die, not sacrificing truth, the guarantee of writing's *authenticity*, for the subterfuge of fiction—has been, for both of these very distinct styles of creation, my avaricious tendency to remain quasi-viscerally attached to my own sentient self as the center and measure of all.

◇

The first time that guileless Don Juan deceived her (a breach that would soon prove to be only the first of many such debacles), it was because of an outfit that was too hastily chosen and of a style that didn't suit him: after that blunder (which hadn't escaped the eye of his companion, already critical of the very Parisian house he had recently purchased) he needed to reassure her by proving that, whether or not he was well or badly dressed, he wasn't a bad-looking man. What's more—and this was the worst part—he hadn't even felt comfortable in that outfit whose elegance departed from his usual look and, feeling as awkward in mind as he did in body, he sensed that this alteration, albeit purely superficial and active only when he was dressed as such, had a sneaky effect on his romantic nature, which was from then on tainted, twisted, devious, and only barely concealed . . . It would have been easy for him—too much of a rich bohemian to worry about waste—to give up wearing the undesirable coat. But a serendipitous encounter pointed him towards a more radical solution: instead of returning to the person he thought he had been and correcting, by trashing the outfit and making a more judicious choice, the annoying mistake that, despite its triviality, was thought to be barely less pernicious than a sin he had purposely committed, he refused to let it go and—pushing the transformation to the extreme in a headlong rush—sought to find not only the approbation he was missing but the security of a new identity in a another woman's love. To create a completely *new skin*—something that he repeatedly had a wide array of excuses for pursuing as the years went by, he who (like many others, whether rich or poor) never felt entirely at ease in his own skin.

Rather than a marked taste for libertinism, a ridiculous wardrobe mistake (a too-revealing jacket and a too-tight vest) was hence the point of departure for this roué, about whom amateur gossips said that he changed women as often as he changed his shirt.

◇

—Call me your Iroquois, your Vandal, your Hun, your Visigoth, your Ostrogoth. . .

—Shut up, you marauder!

—Whatever you say. . . you will always be my travel agency.

$$\diamond$$

Was it from the voyage he made as a seventeen-year-old apprentice aboard the cargo ship *Le Havre et Guadeloupe* to Rio de Janeiro, the city of the legendary carnival, that Édouard Manet brought back—in the many-chambered coffer of his memory—the black figure that, fourteen years later, he would place, charged with a large bouquet and her bare forehead bound in a madras, next to the bed of the white Olympia?

Flush with a warmly spiced exoticism, in a certainly Parisian locale, the only other exotic note—the only allusion tied to an *elsewhere* while the rest is presented under the sign of the here and now—is the female nudity that, in the absence of any sentiment expressed by her face or body, was made for the deliverance of the embrace. . .

For the woman who earned her living typing all day, her greatest joy was to turn, at night, into a clavier played by her lover.

From the day when—in a scandal that was quickly quashed—that older man molested, but not in a violent way, a minor, he was unable to leave his house and stroll around the neighborhood without becoming the object of sidelong glances or disapproving stares. Still, he felt more pride than shame when he considered that he had had enough independence of mind to violate, if not the young girl with pink ribbons in her hair (whom he only wanted, in good faith, to lavish with kindness), at least the taboo protecting children against the precipitous instigators that expose them, as children, to practices that will become normal once they have come of age.

Which is why, even in the face of persistent pillorying, this Hercules with the long, debonair beard, as tall as a cathedral whose only flying buttress was his cane, never tried to make himself as transparent as a sylph or unobtrusive as a Lilliputian. And besides, why should he reproach himself for having wanted to rediscover paradise through the intervention of someone who would, in the present, provide him with a reflection of his own childhood that had been drowned in the ancestral beard with which age had endowed him, age from which he deemed it futile to feign an escape?

◇

Hard like porphyry and curved like an urn, the word "porno" is too beautiful for what it describes: while that abbreviation's stiff and rounded plentitude suggests the highest forms of eroticism, it is familiarly used to designate its most trivial and commercial aspects.

This divergence of form and content is already ubiquitous in the dictionary, a book one is often tempted to conclude is written for the deaf, and in which the arbitrary is so pervasive that common usage seems to have conveniently chosen, from every possible meaning, the least expected option. And yet, the devotee of words needn't revolt, for the correlations this code refuses usually establish themselves through the sins we all commit when we allow ourselves to be swept away by music, and the words the bad shepherd himself had led astray are returned to the straight and narrow path.

Lit without knowing it by invisible tongues of flame, who will rehabilitate the word "porno," which rings as pure and naked as the word "vulve" [vulva], the word "cul" [ass] and the word "burnes" [balls], the last of which is truly filthy in the mouths of honest men?

An enemy of discriminatory practices and wanting there to be no sad sacks among words, the writer endowed with a lofty professional conscience assumed the responsibility of using them all (nobles as well as plebes, pariahs as well as permissibles) and, clearing the forest, checked off in a dictionary each of the ones he had used.

◇

Fear promoted to "anguish,"
dryness "rigor,"
cowardice "weakness,"
inertia "serenity,"
laziness "nonchalance,"
vanity "pride,"
arousal "ardor,"
indifference "insight."

    Underprivileged,
    domestic worker,
    single mother,
    middle age.

◇

Citizens,
comrades,
companions,
brothers,

         beware!

In the West as in the East, we are brainwashed by the mass media to an extreme. Brazen or devious propaganda, advertisements drilled into your head, or catechism: by which ogre would you prefer to be eaten?

By way of press, radio, and television, deluging you with news items that—even if they aren't falsified—pass as *facts* but, flattened realities, are nothing more than verbiage or imagery, you are anesthetized, you are emasculated! Gutenberg, if it is true that you invented that first medium of mass circulation, the printing press, shouldn't you have been sent to the gallows?

As for us, the masses: we swallow the slop offered to us daily without retching, all the fat of sporting events and crime reports seasoned with diversions written too often by simpletons. As for the intelligentsia: wrapping themselves up in major systems, some speak jargon while others, under the pretense of shedding light on the subject and avoiding discourse's uncertainties and abuses of power, expend so many words talking about words that language speaks only for itself, and loses itself in a labyrinth. If we continue along this path, I wonder if, in several years, a mental oasis might emerge that would be exempt from the ravages of these two plagues: the degradation of language and—hardly less deleterious because it is more subtle and hence more rare—its exhaustion by an excess of polish or running around in circles. Audiovisual schoolmaster and popular comic strip, you are equally to blame, for each of you in your own way damages the living practice of thought by encouraging the mind to function as a marginal child.

The anesthesia has an inevitable progression (the only one: it is irrelevant that we live longer—life passes just as quickly; we enjoy more commodities, but our appetites only increase—irrelevant too is our more positive view of our condition, the inhuman cult of Progress replacing that of our fallen gods), but is that an excuse to use any means necessary to dumb us down without, consciously, our rearing up?

Citizens,
comrades,
companions,
brothers,
            beware!

But if my argument is eloquent enough—in all this chaos—to find its way to your ears, beware of me as well, a windbag who issues warnings but has no solutions to propose. Not even, for want of a plan of action, a private strategy of the imaginary, suitable territory for an uncontrollable guerilla. . .

◇

My darling,

You are not here and—short or tall, slender or strong, in shadow or in sunlight—you will never again be there for me. Absent because of my own absence and, neither dead nor alive, an indescribable reflection of that absence. For, already, I only exist elsewhere. . . But where is that? In the desire and regret that oppress me like a curse to which I am delivered, a stranger to myself, bound hand and foot? In the nervous anticipation of the improbable moment when, finding myself again, I will know that I am ready to find you somewhere other than in an idea, a nameless she-devil, without features, without flesh, but of an incomparable attraction? Or in the words that I assemble, despairingly, to fill the void that has consumed me bit by bit?

Be then my muse without face or figure, my darling, and no longer my demon, if it's through what's missing that a muse, once called by our hunger, may sneak in!

P.S. My "darling" who, a plural Eve, is perhaps not only the image that my irritable senses would at times like to make their companion, but—Adam's rib—a buried thing so far away I can barely manage to perceive it, a thing I carry inside myself and that must pass from inside to out, diffuse to compact, for it to escape from Gehenna. An arduous task, if no present-tense delirium can melt me into another (that vulnerable skin I feel: is it mine? is it yours?) and—transforming myself body and soul in its delicious presence—wrest me from the magma of the past, future, and conditional that sickens me, a lukewarm mixture of nostalgia, too-hypothetical hope, and fear.

Golden fleece,
the Seal,
the Otter,
the Honeybee,
the Dragonfly,
the Viper,
the Woodpigeon,
the Lamprey,
Betty Froment,
Girder,
the Gleaner,
the Road,
the Rascal,
the Sibyl,
the Diligent,
the Wise,
the Madwoman,
the Dreamer,
the Tiller,
Viviane,
Morgana,
Radegund,
Clotilde,

Margot,
Violet,
Anonymous,
the Vampire.

Olympia, not a goddess, but a girl of her time, announced as much by the bouquet, still wrapped in its paper and brought to her by the amiable negress in the white dress who is escorted by a beautiful black cat, as by the ornaments—a thin black ribbon at her neck, a large pink bow in her hair, earrings, bracelet, and mules—that distinguish her from what a modern music-hall poster would advertise as "all-nude" and that only make her more enticing.

The salacious angle: clearly a venal girl, and more *real* because of it (according to the terminology that, in the era of the Fréhels and Damias, described as "realistic" the singer whose voice was alleged to be a streetwalker's).

The luxurious angle: an ornament with no soul other than her charm, a girl-puppet as white and as cold as her name suggests, evoking Olympus and the adventures of its gods less than the creature with whom the hero of the Hoffmanian story, *The Sandman*, becomes infatuated to the point of madness and who—vividly alive and attractive as she seems to him, who sees in her something entirely other than a pure artistic effect—proves to be nothing more than an automaton endowed with an overwhelming power of illusion by the doctor who tenuously brought her to life.

◇

*—If I were your sharp-clawed cockerel, you'd cry cock-a-doo-
dle-doo. . .*

Shoes already cast aside on the carpet, and stripped of the
stockings that were as pale as her skin, she took off her dress in
one swift stroke and he thought he saw a curtain rising on a
splendor that blinded him for a moment: this body, giving him
entrance to a fairy tale more marvelous and intense than any of
the spectacles that he saw, or that were read to him, as a child.
Provided, however, that his body, more humble than the other's
even though equally naked, would be able to use with all
required strength and wisdom the magic wand with which, for a
time, his sensual fury had armed him.

. . .And whatever else you have to say will be told by your breath!

◇

At the sight of his member, as long, thin, and straight as a pole, she saluted with her arm outstretched horizontally and flourishing into an open palm, a sort of Olympic salute recalling that of the young blonde trapeze artist whose back flared out in a fan from her slender hips to her larger, elegantly drawn shoulders and who one night that previous summer, perched nearly naked on the narrow platform where she was taking a short rest, grabbed the trapeze with her left hand to pay homage—extending her right arm toward him, unfolding it as if she were taking an oath or preparing for an impending leap while she turned her majestic profile in the same direction—to one of her colleagues who had just performed, in the heights of the circus tent and under the harsh glare of the spotlights, a marvelous tour de force: a leap of death, or something like it.

◇

Whether or not Édouard Manet intended it, his *Olympia* is arranged like stems of the sumptuous bouquet of carnal love gathered together in the cramped room that provides its setting:

the object of desire (Olympia, whose ribbon and other accessories only emphasize her nudity);

the call to passions foreign to ordinary, everyday life (the dark-skinned chambermaid dressed for a different climate);

the obscurity of a mystery that allows itself to be touched but cannot be diminished by a caress (the black cat).

◇

For the innocent she had conquered, the bitch spared nothing: when she came, she let him know that it wasn't he but his sex who had thrilled her, found worthy by chance of the fiery mare that she was.

◇

Sometimes during those solitary hours of morose ecstasy in which anguish finds a provisional escape by becoming desire, my stand-in, that ageless double at once myself and not at all myself that displaces me in my dreams, likes to plan—craving the enclosed totality of an island—the final scene as follows: after making himself androgynous by offering his naked torso to the caresses of his own palms, he manipulates his prick encircled by his left hand with a languid up-and-down motion and, with the right, grips the butt of a revolver whose barrel he places on his temple and pulls the trigger at exactly the second when the solid ejection of the bullet coincides with that, liquid, of his semen.

Barely visible, scarcely more than the earrings we assume are equally expensive, the delicate gem fastened to the black ribbon at the neck of the resting Olympia. Whether or not we notice it hardly matters: the room's jewel box—which seems to be almost entirely taken up by the bed of its inhabitant—contains no other treasure than that very one whose flesh the precious pendant might enrich if it weren't already highlighted by more modest foils but that leaps out from the work as it was, if not envisioned, as least manually realized.

◇

It was probably because I was in Venice and not at home when the idea arose in my sleeping mind, in a short scene set outside of Paris (although probably not very far away) whose principal actor was an Italian friend (by name if not by nationality), that Alberto Giacometti and I were traveling together or came across each other during a train departure or a changing of trains. And perhaps it was the environment in which I was spending my days at the time—having found myself in the classical city of masked carnivals and dominoes for the 1963 holidays, a city that has for some time now become a tourist attraction filled with foreigners dressed in God knows what and who sometimes don't hesitate, the women at any rate, to don headgear that imitates the gondoliers—that caused Giacometti (whom I have only ever seen helmeted by savagely fluffy curls, crowning a face whose stony complexion appears to be a response to his occupation as a sculptor) to wear an extremely elegant bowler hat with a narrow brim, almost like a soft felt hat, while I myself sported a Cronstadt, the kind that existed almost a century ago, but in gray instead of black, or a kind of squat top hat that was matte instead of glossy gray.

It must also have been because Venice—a city favorable to rendezvous, intrigues, and long, gossipy stoppings-off at café terraces—was there in the background that Giacometti told me about how he was very much in love with a woman and had asked about her to Édouard Pignon (a painter who was our contemporary and who, because of his robust physique and head crested with copper hair that has since faded, always made me think of a fighting cock like those in the north of France, where he is originally from). About the woman, whom he presumably knew well enough to make a peremptory judgment, Pignon had said (tactlessly, in Giacometti's opinion, as he had been hurt by his comments): "The Green Fly: she's a bargain."

A bargain: in other words, something like a reject. But why the Green Fly? And what was behind that peculiar sobriquet with a slightly creepy twist? Each time this dream returned to me, I wondered . . . Until the day when—I don't know how—I learned that the cantharide, whose properties in powdered form are well known, is green. I wish I could refer to my source, as I had a doubt when I found (while seeking confirmation) that my dictionary lacked any indication of the insect's appearance and noted only that it is commonly known as the "Spanish fly."

If I were to consult an entomology book, the question would be quickly resolved. But, being either too lazy or too sensible to search through a book that could provide the answer to this frivolous question, I fall back on the notion that since nothing in my dictionary contradicted that the blister beetle or Spanish fly is essentially a green fly, I have no reason to doubt it. Besides, I don't think that's the main issue, since the strange thing was that as it happened—thanks to some obscure intuition or some sudden remembrance of a forgotten fact?—I hadn't needed to know the exact meaning of the "Green Fly" to appropriate it as an imaginary piece of slander. How strong, I think, throwing my scruples overboard, the erotic attraction must have been of this woman Giacometti loved so much and that Pignon called a slut, granting her—through the name which, out of defiance, she had perhaps given herself as a *nom de guerre*, as if she were putting on a provocatively colored costume—the traits that allowed this woman with a checkered past to be identified with an aphrodisiac considered to be just as noxious as the pestilent, anthrax-infested fly that as a child I confused with the large blue common house-fly with a metallic sheen!

Alberto Giacometti has left us. As for Édouard Pignon, I note—pleased to see fantasy's teeth-marks on reality in it—that not too long ago he painted a series of *Red Nudes* as if, in a game of complementaries, he had wanted to create a counterpoint to the Green Fly who appeared in a dream that was not even his own and about which he knew nothing.

But when will the Green Fly quit nagging at me? Just this minute, I remember that Giacometti made a connection in an old piece of writing between having gonorrhea and dreaming about a yellow spider. From the venereal yellow spider to the Venusian or Venetian? green fly, the distance is not great, and so I certainly could have, without making too great a leap, passed from one to another in my sleep.

◇

Early for an art opening I was planning to take a look at, having known and admired the artist for many years even though, since I was primarily friends with other members of his clique, I rarely saw him even in the old days and knew very little about him personally—that he had made a trip, while young and short of money, to Tahiti (something I learned about recently from a mutual friend who took me to see his drawings that were inspired by that fallen paradise), along with one other detail I then remembered, the beautiful voice of this easygoing, decent guy who had worn himself out living hand-to-mouth, whose desire for a change of scene had impelled him to dive into the mirage of the islands, something that, having not always lived a sedentary lifestyle myself, I could appreciate—I settled in, to kill some time and escape from an unpleasant autumn rain, at the Frigate, a café-restaurant on the quays near my publishing house in the very bourgeois 17th arrondisement. In the past, when the establishment was still just a café, I went there from time to time to meet up with some friend or other whose passions and interests I shared. But, as the years have stretched friendships thin and (in a more radical break) eliminated companions at a brutal, nauseating rate, I no longer have many such rendezvous these days, and so It's been a long time since I visited this place whose atmosphere might be called provincial if the cafés in the provinces weren't so often just as noisy as their Parisian counterparts.

Other than its name, which could perhaps be explained by its proximity to the Seine, I can find only one juncture through which fantasy might allow the idea of navigation to infiltrate this peaceful Frigate: the trapdoor that occasionally, without anyone having visibly flipped its invisible switch, slowly opens out from the café floor and through which heavy cases of bottles rise up in silence from the cellar on a carousel so mysterious and ominous that it would hardly be a stretch to suppose that the cellar was filled, like a buccaneer's stash, with tafia casks, barrels of gunpowder, and other supplies.

Sitting at a small table in this half-deserted locale, in a chair whose seat and curved backrest are covered in leather and that, as I think about it again now, could easily grace the lounge of a ship, I drink a Guinness. Perched on the back of the neighboring chair, a suitable and certainly comfortable seat, is a large, napping cat, if I judge correctly by his closed eyes. A fat cat, like a galleyman's cat, I think, again striking the chord of maritime adventure novels. When he tires of his position, or, having finished sleeping, instinctively recognizes me as another mammal who might serve as his companion, he emerges from his torpor, jumps onto my lap, and pushes his head under the left lapel of my jacket in increments, sinking so deeply into the tunnel he has hollowed out that I fear, given the animal's size, he will pop the button that keeps my jacked closed. A ridiculous but irritating mishap that I protect myself against by freeing the disc made of galalith or some other hard material from its buttonhole in order to spare the strand that fastens it from the prolonged strain it would have to endure.

In a search for contact or a desire to stay warm, the cat nestled in my lap persists in thrusting his head against me and burying his head under my jacket, like a baby who suckles under the modest cloak that allows his wet nurse to hide the operation.

Drinking the caramelly, opaque brown beer in small sips that is served colder here than what custom dictates across the Channel, I pet the little meddler and scratch his head, pleased by the trust he placed in me almost as if it were a sign of good luck.

In a brighter mood than when I arrived and, despite the discouraging weather, setting out once again on my route at a leisurely pace, I went to the opening on the other side of the river. But, since I arrived too early for the party and stayed no longer than what a thorough visit required, I roamed the cramped rooms where the paintings were hung without finding a living soul, except for two or three strangers, figures who had for me neither history nor depth.

◇

"Outlying" and, even worse, "peripheral" would be terrible epithets to describe that area of Paris; although far from the city and difficult to get to, we should rather say, "forgotten," since other areas—more frequented than it, which is neither commercial nor residential and is completely undeveloped—are separated from it by barricades. I know that to get there you have to take a tramway and that at the end of this tramway, fairly high up (and I'm speaking here of a mountain whose hills are more extensive and steep than La Butte or the neighboring Galette and Sacre-Coeur) I will be able to recognize, from the features of the houses and the way they are arranged, a spot close to my destination that I will have to reach on foot. It's a long haul, and I still have a long way to go; my house is miles from where the tramway begins, a distance that will have to be crossed on the métro or some other means of transportation. I have a lingering memory of a métro station, probably in Montmartre or on the outskirts of Montmartre, located next to a flight of stairs that it cheers up by resembling a glittery boutique or corner store, bursting at the seams with goods whose colors recall the kaleidoscopic mass of prints and items sold by the merchants whom many métro stations host in their corridors but, spread out in the open air, are more directly reminiscent of the bunches of sweets and toys that small vendors in public parks display in their pavilions.

I'm unable to remember the name of this station when, in the middle of the night (four in the morning, wintertime) and half asleep, I recapitulate this dream and try to resolve one question in particular: is this neighborhood, where the slope of a large mountain rises first towards the north and then the east and ends not far from the Ivry or Bercy warehouses, the neighborhood near where I get off the tramway (or the second tramway, really, since once I'm almost halfway there I have to change), that featureless neighborhood probably located just past—or just before?—an area that, on an old map, seems to be almost as empty as a *terra incognita*, is this an actual district of Paris or is it, like the enormous wasteland of the quasi-deserted zone that is crossed—or bypassed?—by the tramway line, an imaginary district I dreamt about but that, perhaps, I did not invent because, perhaps, it had already manifested in other dreams and, perhaps, this dream—or rather this rumination regarding a trip I had already made but that this time, while trying to recreate it, I followed only in my imagination—allowed me to discover it again by reintroducing myself into the parallel world to which it belonged? A district endowed, as a result, with a sort of existence and that simply would have concerned a topography other than that of my waking life.

My thoughts centered for a fairly long time, I think, on this problem whose most difficult point of clarification was the métro station, which was less obviously aberrant than the tramway, a mode of locomotion that has been obsolete in Paris for many years (a detail I realized in the morning, and from which I deduced that the lost Parisian district to which the tramway led was not an actual district). Once the illusion had dissipated, I wondered for a moment if I shouldn't actually try to find out which métro station this might have been, since it is quite possible that one like it existed in Paris. However, idleness and self-respect won out: considering it tedious and ridiculous to look on a map—checking off all of the stations that, by their location, on the right bank and close to Montmartre, could be the one in my dream, "Notre-Dame-de-Lorette," "Saint-Georges," "Château-Rouge," for example—and then carry out what would certainly have been multiple trips seeking definite verification, I abandoned the idea, more and more convinced besides that the métro station—as charming as a Christmas tree trimmed with lights and toys, in the center of a bustling city, halfway up a staircase full of comings and goings—could only have been a fantasy that rose straight from my sleep.

◇

King with no kingdom,
Queen with no court,
Castle cracked
Bishop beaten
Knight crestfallen.

◇

Eyes closed, I can see—through the somnolence I've fallen into from the heat of the water that fills my bathtub three-quarters full and the head cold that's been plaguing me for two days—a character from the Middle Ages, probably from the religious wars. Knees bent as he walks, this strapping man with a thick head of hair, short beard and thick mustache, all three as black as his close-fitting cassock and hose, drags a giant gold necklace along the grassy edge of a road or muddy path, like a fisherman dragging across the sand a net that he had pulled up from the sea.

No sound of clashing rapiers, no alarm bell of Saint-Germain-l'Auxerois. Only the vision, like a snapshot, of this frozen tableau whose most fascinating element is the way the necklace—thin but too inordinately long for any human creature to be able to wear it around the neck—superimposes its double row of finely wrought chain, in truth a single chain curling in on itself, over the slightly bleached-out, pale green of the relatively tall grass in the background.

Aurea catena . . . So begins (the only words I remember) the title of a book on the occult that I once found a mention of somewhere—back when I was entranced by the sumptuous imagery produced by that genre of philosophy—that dates, I believe, from the seventeenth or eighteenth century. Out of sync, then, with the earlier century (the sixteenth, fictive age of Henry II's buffets) to which, according to his appearance at least, the man seemed to belong, a kind of swashbuckler or accursed huntsman transporting a heavy load, perhaps more cumbersome than it was heavy, an extensive and priceless series of links that I knew was a necklace, but which offered no visible clasp to my inner eye.

And yet, this discrepancy did not prohibit me from suspecting the existence of a filiation between the *Aurea catena* and my "gold chain," so close to each other in name!

In the early morning, between waking and sleep, it's rare for me not to be seized by a dizzy spell while I'm still dreaming. As the fathomless nature of these truly poignant spells seems to suggest, growing old and dying—the essence of the anxiety to which, once awake, I will fall prey—are likely the bedrock of these slack and disagreeable thoughts, so evanescent and of such a bizarre subtlety that I can't remember even a single one to cite as an example. Ordinarily—and I know nothing more about it than this—I worry about two things of the same species that I must choose between or that, representing two terms of a dilemma, call for a weighing of *for* and *against*, a paradox that seems to contain a question whose prospect (even without any sign of impending disaster) torments me, but that is too inevitable a fatality to be a matter of a distinction or a dilemma. Perhaps I am substituting uncertainty for my perpetual anxiety, as if being perplexed, without removing my anguish, could allow me to minimize it and hence play the role of a relative diversion. Anguish that is profoundly my own, but that I cannot regard as belonging solely to me, motivated as it is by that very thing that, the basis of every religion and root of the tyrannical need to busy oneself in one way or another, darkens the horizon of the phrases the lucid writer uses to avoid the concept, even when he explicitly addresses it and even though, by transplanting himself into the immaterial field of language, he is training himself to die.

I managed to recover (or to believe I had recovered), after great effort, two of these early morning dilemmas, probably because they were the simplest and hence least difficult to reconstruct:

for (supposedly) a contentious passage in a text I was working on the night before, which word do I choose between two that mean the same or nearly the same thing but which one—and here I procrastinate without finally making a decision—would be, if not more fitting, at least more beautifully wrought than the other?

between two possible vacation spots, one of which is a modest, sturdy house in the country, and the other—more sophisticated although the country house is that as well—a hotel-restaurant with a terrace that looks like a dance hall with electric lamps (because it's night-time) that light up the trees, which should I choose if I need to leave Paris to rest for several days?

This last dilemma is particularly inane—a frivolous question, and a purely theoretical one besides, since it relates to a judgment and not a choice that would be followed by a result—and seems to me, with its house reduced or almost reduced to the idea of "house" and its crude chromolithograph as a counterpoint, to be a living illustration of life's inanity.

◇

Arrived, I think, by car. Not at a lodge, but maybe some kind of inn, or what is commonly known as a "bouchon"? At any rate, we find ourselves in front of a copse with large, serrated leaves so green and rich that they obstruct any view of the horizon.

The route through the forest involves a fairly long hike, uphill, but not too steep. The trail is interrupted by several streams that we must wade through. Just as I did for the first, I begin to swim across the last with several strokes that are especially awkward, as I am weighed down by heavy camping clothes and a raincoat with a thick removable lining. A local boy tells me I can touch bottom there and that, while standing up, the water will only come up to my thighs. But when I try, I realize that it is almost up to my chest and that in this new position I will have to struggle to resist the current.

Some time before, near the trail's halfway mark, we come across a half-dead dog, a German shepherd we only acknowledge after we're twenty meters away and whose coat, a handsome, solid color, is a slightly tawny beige. Probably lost because of the flooding caused by the rising streams, and likely starving, he lies on his belly and, without trying to stand up on his paws, seems to want to bury himself in the mud his muzzle is pointing towards. We feel bad for the poor thing, but what can we do? I myself have a twinge of anxiety—when we see the dog again on the way back down (which is likely, given that she is in such bad shape), will she have become rabid?

Finally, I notice—marked by a kind of mast (a meteorological or radio tower, or maybe just a pole)—a low summit with a very slightly rounded cap of bare earth that, beyond the forest, must be the end point of our excursion, or it could at least be its logical conclusion: once we reach this culminating point, there's no reason to go any further. I'm also pleased by the thought that soon we won't have to exert ourselves any longer, but only go back down the hill.

From that point on, I consider the venture to be over. . . But suddenly, at that exact moment, someone knocks sharply at the door. It's our morning tea, brought as it is every day by the wife of our friendly Moroccan servant, signaling that the time has come to satisfy the desire that had troubled my sleep towards its end and posed, underhandedly, that question that I know—by experience—can wear the most hypocritical disguises: do I get up to piss, or do I wait?

Right away, I take great satisfaction in noting a perfect concordance between my waking up and the end of the trail. That life begins again exactly at the natural conclusion of a dream instead of senselessly interrupting it is a triumph analogous to the kind of miracle represented by a death that, arriving unexpectedly, is almost tolerable because it is well-timed.

◇

Between the golden yellow object (gleaming like a saffron ingot) and the steel gray object (rough and dull), the choice is simple. But, as it happens, I don't have to choose: the yellow gold, in its gala costume, is not meant for everyone and it is quite possible that, of the two objects, so unequal in content but analogous in form (although the edges of the second are more accentuated than those, rounded, of the first), the steel gray will be the one that belongs to me and that—according to whatever criteria or whatever reason—ranks me below the elite. Of course, the yellow object is much more attractive, but I contemplate becoming satisfied with the steel gray without bitterness. There's nothing to argue about when I haven't a choice, and I cannot honestly create a drama, even though one may exist, out of the opposition of these two objects, or out of the uncertainty into which I am thrown by not knowing which term of a pair, equals in a certain sense but whose aspects and values are dissimilar, belongs to me.

◇

The gorgeous light after the storm: an engine well-oiled by the rain, putting each thing in its exact place without jerk or squeak. What immeasurable joy (while its cause may be modest) is given by the sight, immutable but of a color so warm one might imagine an impending explosion, of everything it carves out in luminous serrations!

Three trees who are my friends and who, since I can see them more clearly then, are closer friends in winter than in summer. Three trees whom, unilaterally, I often meet, since they are principal landmarks on my Friday walks through the woods and fields. Three trees whom I could then consider as friends but whose names I do not even know, being ignorant of botany and, even worse, I wouldn't even be able to tell you if they are exactly the same kind. (As for their names, it goes without saying that this would only be a matter of their family name, since animals capable or supposedly capable of responding when their names are called are the only living souls to be granted this rudiment of the civil state.)

Even when they stir and rustle in the wind, I know that these trees aren't speaking to me, and that they send me no sign. But they are there, in whatever season it may be, and they assure me that I myself am there as well—someone who, being of this world as much as them, rediscover them from time to time, when I have the leisure to look and respond to their presence. Too near to me and and too much like an adventitious organ, not even a piece of furniture or another familiar instrument— an object devoid of any semblance of a soul, even though I may personalize it—gives me such consistent reassurance, grounded on a feeling of reunion.

Of these three (or rather of these two, since the tallest is far-ther away from the two others than the two others are from each other) there is one, the smaller one, who—stooping over—looks a bit like a sad sack who has grown old before his time or been afflicted by some disgrace. This is certainly not the one I like best; I like the tallest one. Not because he is a giant (he would have to be much taller for that), but because, close to the ground, his trunk—whose base contains a twist on one side that foreshadows its eventual bursting—divides in two (one of the halves almost immediately splitting off on its own in such a way that it appears to divide into three sections from the foundation) and because its burden of branches, when stripped of their leaves instead of disappearing into a muddled blur, scrawls an inky black signature over the sky with a daring and panache that the other two do not possess.

CELTIC STELE. Erected in Scotland or Ireland, coldly geometric and lacking the contoured detail that would permit us to count it among one of the strange images of the natural world that may have inspired the legend of Lot's wife changing into a pillar of salt after turning around, not towards a Eurydice for whom she was an Orpheus, but towards the fire that destroyed Sodom and Gomorrah, or anything that would confer upon it a commemorative or funereal character, anything that in the final analysis would qualify it as an *omegalith*, assuming that a stone, large in size but not unrefined, could be seen as a kind of megalith. Parallelepiped that flanks—close on the left and the right sides and slightly in front of, from the observer's point of view—two other, slightly smaller parallelepiped sitting horizontally on the ground in the way that gravestones, fragments of ancient architecture now destroyed, or cinderblocks from a construction site might have been. Neither building blocks for a future edifice, nor debris from ancient monuments, nor receptacles for the remains that human life leaves behind and a cemetery unites, these two sharp-edged, solid forms look to me like *beds of stone* even though they are, in truth, something other than beds: sleeping bags that the body slips inside rather than furniture it stretches out on like a recumbent statue.

Not far from these two monoliths—much greater in volume but almost the same shape as the bars of salt that, in Ethiopia, were once used as currency and transported by caravan on the backs of mules—a slightly beatnik-looking couple, perhaps young snobs pretending to belong to that marginal class that appears to have for its ideal the adoption of a lifestyle as crude as that of those who lived in medieval times. Clothes made of worn-out, patchwork, faded fabric, long hair on the women (hanging straight down or tied together by a band that might very well be nothing more than a piece of string); thick hair and beards on their male companions. I know nothing about these future denizens of the beds of stone except that they're wearing blue jeans that look fairly clean and that, svelte, bright, and certainly beautiful, they are of different sexes. Sleeping with sheets or a blanket made of stone would certainly be unusual, but a bed of stone—a lithic couch upon which the traveller may enjoy a short nap—is easier to imagine than the *festin de pierre* that is the subtitle of Molière's *Don Juan* and that once when I was young, not knowing that "festin" meant "guest," I associated with the muddled image of a granite table on which a meal would have been served.

More sandy than rocky was the lair belonging to Tanguy the farm hand, a drunk and semi-vagrant Breton who served as the efficient assistant to our gardener for many years. He didn't have a stone scabbard for a bed, but he did have a kind of burrow he had found ready-made that was the perfect size for him to sleep in, fully dressed, after wrapping himself up in newspaper when winter required him to protect himself from the cold. An old motorcycle, some kitchen utensils, a stack of firewood prepared for burning in the open air, along with a bundle of old newspapers and magazines that comprised what he called his "library"—that was nearly everything this Diogenes possessed. That he was defiant, ferociously attached to his freedom, and a philosopher if ever there was one was proved to me one day among many others when I urged him to go to the village clinic to take care of a wound to his toe (due, he thought, to a rat bite he had gotten while sleeping in his hole) which had pained him for some time and now to such a degree that he was walking around with the afflicted foot bare, being unable to wear shoes after enduring the torture of his work boots—pain that he nevertheless endured instead of exposing himself to the risk of hospitalization by going to the clinic for treatment. "What good is a toe?" he said to me, a rigorously functional and cynical insight that was just as much his way as was the naked toe. And whether it illustrated Gallic humor or attic salt, his declaration shut my mouth. . .

◇

At the very end of the narrow road that cuts through the forest, I noticed, pink in the autumn light, a slice of the red brick roof that I know—having seen it up close many times while passing through this area—covers a hangar that houses agricultural machines. But seen from a distance and glimpsed from the bottom of the horizontal shaft of light breaking through the tree-filled space, the parcel of roof whose remainder was hidden from view did not appear to be the fragment of a utilitarian structure at all, but rather—and this was a surprise—part of a pavilion where undefinable joys awaited me and whose illusory sight would already procure for me, by doing nothing more than simply pointing to the idea of the pavilion, a brief moment of perfect joy. To be sure, the promised joys I imagined would not have included waffles or any of those solid or liquid confections that children take such delight in after they've finished their games, and yet, because of these childhood memories, they would have provided me with everything tonic and delectable that the word "pavilion" suggests, along with the image whose vaporous contours it instantly conjures: an aerial structure in keeping with the mosque, the nomadic tent, and the carousel.

While smoking a cigarette and drinking tea in my bedroom in Paris, the desire often strikes me—irrational but acutely felt—to smoke a cigarette. But I am already smoking, and thus it is absurd to wish to do something that, quite simply, I'm in the middle of doing. Probably, what I actually want is the sense of peace that the act of smoking provides (holding the Rothman in between the index and middle fingers of my right hand with my right elbow resting on my left palm, raising it to my mouth and deeply inhaling the smoke, detaching the filtered side from my lips and then expelling the smoke, preferably through my nostrils, occasionally substituting the thumb for the index finger so it can flick the ash from the tip with two slight taps on the incandescent end of the cylinder, causing the ash to fall into the garish 1900 ashtray decorated by the profile of a young girl in relief looking out with her eyes raised towards the sky, appearing to emerge from the double wave of never-ending tresses encircling the thick shallow chalice made of metal.) But the peace I was counting on when I lit the cigarette with my lighter did not take effect, and since I remain in the exact same state I had hoped to put an end to by smoking, I still have the same desire, born of the same feeling of lack, a desire that takes as its object—perhaps a matter of habit causing automatism?—that thing that I'm already doing and that, inoperative, leaves the desire intact—a desire for relief that should rationally steer me towards something other than the ineffective palliative I'm already applying.

For a moment, I'm so entirely preoccupied by this desire that it doesn't cross my mind that, smoking and dreaming of smoking as if I weren't already smoking, my desire has as its object something that I need not desire because I am, presently, fulfilling it and anyway, the desire is absurd for an entirely different reason: its persistence demonstrates the uselessness of this thing that cannot fulfill it, despite the short, faint pleasure it may provide. When, almost immediately, I discover that the thing I want to do is exactly the thing that I'm doing, but that satisfying my desire like this, in a minor form, leaves it unsatisfied, I'm mortified by my absentmindedness as a sign of cerebral erosion, but most of all I feel slightly dizzy, sensing that, even if I have not being entirely awake as an excuse, a fissure exists there: one that will continue to exist deep down while, on the surface, my desire will have been fulfilled.

◇

That stubborn man who, to sniff out intoxicating truths or at least to satisfy a tyrannical desire to inebriate himself, depended on his pen the way a wizard depends on his wand could, at last, consider himself a literary success. But that success—limited, when all is said and done, and far from promising him the kind of glory that would assure his beneficiaries any semblance of a means of survival—was perhaps even more crushing than failure. What could he conclude from this misfire, if not that he must correct it and immediately try his luck once again? And so this kind of success—or what may seem like it to a few others—leaves him face to face with this irreparable fact: the observation that to have played and apparently won hadn't, in the end, led to much in terms of what—originally—had motivated him. From there, saying that victory or defeat are one and the same is not a great leap and, having taken it, he struggled to rid himself of this constraint: the idea that nothing is worth breaking your back over.

(It's at such a moment that, incorrigibly obstinate, I grab hold of the ribbon at *Olympia*'s throat, the rope that keeps me from foundering.)

◇

On one side, undulating hills in low relief; on the other, a half-moon formed approximately by the edge of a bay embracing a sea whose only boundary is the horizon line.

Despite this landscape's unarguable beauty, I wouldn't have even remembered admiring it if I hadn't found a trace of it in one of the notebooks to which I devote, without method or continuity—and as a stopgap—whatever (thing or idea) I would like to inscribe in my brain, as if it were a consultable dictionary without even having to be browsed, lines sometimes so brief that after a more or less extended period of time they hardly fulfill their function as a reminder and provide me with, at best, a barely identifiable skeleton of what I had experienced or thought. Thus this landscape that I can hazily evoke when I refer to the mention of it in my notebook but am unable to recreate without a detail to use as a lever (like the ribbon, the handkerchief, or insignificant trinket through which the suitor of yesteryear could, even in her absence, feel his beloved's presence or some bone that, for the paleontologist, becomes the bearer of an abolished world).

Besides, haven't I gradually come to the conclusion that this kind of panorama affects me less, ordinarily, than the limitless view of a savanna, a desert, or even a prosaically cultivated plain that extends out in all directions and envelops me instead of offering itself as a spectacle (to which, spectacle for spectacle, I would prefer a sky tumultuously embossed with clouds)?

It was during a month of August spent on the beach in Brittany, while I was walking—probably during the magic hour—away from the edge of the sea and allowing the coastline whose expanse had drawn me in to slip away, that the traditional sign of the sun—a point surrounded by a circle—appeared to me not as a conventional graphic, but as an image that proposed concrete truths within my reach. The image felt all the more striking because I had just completed a trip to the tropics that had almost led me to conclude that I had parted ways with the sun, whose heat is strong enough in those regions to cause terrible fevers and problems.

Standing upright and casting a shadow that, as time passes, travels around me like the needle of shadow around a sun dial, am I not at the center of the outside world, annular scenery that my eyes reduce to a horizon whose straight line I know to be an illusion, know that in fact it curves until it bites its own tail?

A crown and a scepter, a vulva and a penis, the circle and the point. A newborn king, man emerges head first from the matrix circumscribed by the horizon. A pebble thrown into the originary waters, the point creates a circle, then a series of concentric circles in the water that ripples with the impact. Thrown into the world like a pebble, I may join it in any number of ways but will produce nothing that contributes to it and remain, as long as I live, the creator of my own prison: the horizon (nature's apparent limit) that my fall has drawn around me. That planetary sign I dreamed about while walking in the silky light of the Côtes-du-Nord was a cosmological master, revealing that my situation can only stay the same, despite the displacement of my point and the gradual transformation of my horizon! Its ideogram was so loquacious that I needed no effort of the imagination to also see in this circle, stamped in its center by a shadowy dot, the swelling of a breast, whose communion-wafer roundness had for a soul a point that hardened, in a sort of transubstantiation, with a caress. But isn't this overtly libidinous reading also logically justified, since I am at the *heart* [au sein] of the world, and exist because of it?

Point and circle, center and periphery: myself and what surrounds me, or rather my consciousness and everything, including my body, that seems external to that axis. Even now, this graphic acts as a mold into which I pour various thoughts, all in the same vein although taking different forms: such as a chess piece, a rook, for example, a tall tube of thick masonry with castellations at the top and dungeons below that are so deep that no one knows what they contain, enclosed at a distance by a ring of fortifications, which is itself surrounded—*Defend the tower! Defend the tower!*—by an omnipresent threat that forces me to trust in these fortifications less (for they will too quickly be struck down) than an ultimate retreat, wishing to be invulnerable while understanding the inanity of that wish. Castle, lighthouse, whatever apparently inviolable thing that its surroundings protect, doesn't that encircled point—a sun dispensing rays that go out even before the universe can use their energy and so, it seems to me, like prey surrounded by a pack of dogs or a scalped man tied to a pot surrounded by singing and dancing savages—exemplify, in each of the translations I've given, the last of which (considering only the formal similarity of the schematic) might be counterbalanced by the image of a smiling, blindfolded boy standing at the center of a circle of young girls who tease him, a deeply felt truth that seems to touch upon the essential?

An exact tracing, this time, of the symbol of the sun as a vibrating gong that in its season of glory is successively an alarm clock, a saucepan whose clanging calls us from afar, and a coin that drops every night into who knows what piggy bank, another image that will only appear in time, when the moment arrives to cut the cord attaching me to this récit whose unstable foundations are an Armorican memory: neither wheel nor phonograph record but—in the absence of sound grooves or any indication that listening contains, will contain, or had contained a turning—a target, nailed down at the bullseye the archer must hit to succeed, as I'm trying to do with this sketch—without taking it for anything other than a fragile watercolor inspired by an almost inexistent motif—whose fumbling strokes I would like to be something more than stray bullets, much ado about nothing, or castles in the air.

◇

Forgotten song,
name that's on the tip of your tongue,
drop that the apparently full vase accepts,
hole that forms a vacuum around itself,
lost ring that must perhaps be invented
rather than found or freed from its gangue.

◇

Is it upside down to think the sun orbits around the earth and believe you are at the center of a world created only for you, to feel the effect of a certain generosity of words and things—that would like to be positive and lend themselves to play—as the ability that we sometimes have (although we would like to have it always) to write in such a way that, at least at that moment, we seem to have said something worth being said and to have said it as it ought to have been said? We're helpless when things and words seem hostile to the point of total intransigence and stay as impermeable as stones. Impossible to write a phrase that holds up when every thing and idea bristles, curls into a ball, and refuses to let itself be touched. Ostensibly, it's the world's initiative and not my own that creates the perceptions and feelings I'm immersed in: it's the world's job to issue me a summons, and mine to respond, as long as words agree. If, by chance, the right answer comes, it's by those strokes of luck that some call inspiration. . .

My wish to find friendly collaborators in the things that occupy the outside world (as does, among other things, my body) and in those formless things that, internally, seem like foreign enclaves is so strong that, reversing the roles and forgetting that I am the one who's in charge, I wait for them to give me some sign and dictate, with the connivance of words, the conversation I am meant to have with them. I am on the edge of that madness that treats soliloquy as dialogue—that thinks citizens of other kingdoms—including the kingdom of the unspeakable, which is entirely internal—and language itself could communicate with me through some remarkable stroke of luck. To act as if some element of nature or my urban environment, some example of what I baptize as "things" (extending this term to include any number of accidents caused by my internal geography) had a message for me, delivered from on high; too devoted to language to recognize that before speaking to me it was spoken by me, acting like an instrumentalist hoping that his instrument will, by itself, regale him with music—what an aberration, when I claim to be an idealist! And what laziness, since it expects that a miracle will be fulfilled without, as it were, even lifting a finger!

The only poetry is something that you don't think about and that takes shape on its own. It should be a blind and deaf force. And above all, it must never look back at itself. . . That is what, after banging my head against the wall trying to describe a technique that would be for the poet something like (they say) what ecstatic practices are for Tibetan monks, I wrote down in the multipurpose journal that has its counterpart in a seasonal (spring, summer, autumn, winter) pocket diary, split into four sections, in which I use the immediate future tense, both of which are reassuring memory aids since one, crystallizing the past and reflecting preoccupations that have changed only slightly since, proves to me, when curiosity and the desire for still-virgin material inspires me to refer to it, that I have lived in a more or less coherent fashion until now while the other, using the future tense to mark down a rendezvous or outing I have planned, seems to offer a written promise that I will, at least until that date, still be alive. That assertion—and it seems to me now like a vow of impotence—opting on the whole for a kind of immobility that would allow me to twiddle my thumbs while waiting for poetry to fall from the sky, fully formed—would be the exact opposite, and I conclude from these lines that I was in great distress when I was inclined to write them barely a month ago. Hadn't I, in fact, begun by affirming—as an observer who only studies himself to understand how what he considers to be a rare blessing is produced in him and how, once so informed, he can summon up such moments at will—that when I feel poetry, a filter that amplifies life and doubtless has no other justification, rising up I have the impression *of a kind of revolution being produced within me—a turning movement in which my thinking seems to describe a semicircle and so comes face to face with itself?* Which, taking this face-to-face encounter (whose sovereign lucidity is the opposite of blind surrender) as a primordial condition, I followed with this semblance of a conclusion: *That is how words, instead of being mechanically (psittacismically) arranged, take on color and weight* (acquire the granite density and warm hues that at that time I particularly wished they would have, and quit following one another around in dull, parrot-like chatter); *they move me* (touch me and spur me on as ardent and tender words that culminate in a discernible point inside me) and *no longer count for me as words* (become something other than lifeless tools). And I also said, not letting go of the idea of an internal dynamic that I had written down a moment before in this unpolished form: *to habituate oneself to a certain proliferation of consciousness and oppose it to one's heart* (a romantic and especially imprecise phrase) *as one typically opposes oneself to a tree or a house*, refusing to let go of the buoy of that idea—of facing one's feelings as if facing a palpable object—and trying, far from successfully, both to enlarge the field and seat a conviction that I admit is more visceral than intellectual: *Such a state corresponds less to casting myself out into the outside world than concentrating the outside world within myself. And yet, more than a return from the periphery to the center* (returning to the self after being captivated), *we find identification—without movement in any sense—between the periphery and the center* (no barrier between this "I" who speaks and the circus of tangible realities that surround it near and far away). *It's as if plants were growing out of your chest and the multiplicity of experience were taking birth in your bones.* A fierce aspiration to a dazzling, concrete apprehension, which I haven't relinquished but that, in this case, caused me to lose myself in the mirror games of the penetrating verbal analyst I would like to have been. Such straying proves how much turmoil, which I will do almost anything to alleviate, this apparently technical question causes me: does poetry arise through strategy or blind acquiescence? If I were less disoriented, more fit, and too caught up in practice to worry about theory, I probably would not even have asked the question—even if I actually had posed it in terms of for and against, and it wasn't a mirage, the detached perspective I was able to take while rereading it after it had lain dormant for some time reveals a reversal that, although it was caused by my mood (concluding with an idea that led nowhere), seems, from a distance, to express my uncertainty on a point that, deep down, I have secretly struggled with.

To let it happen, or to try to make something happen, that would be the alternative, and I don't know any more than I did yesterday which path to choose: a kind of passivity (in the past, delivering myself to verbal machinations, today, waiting for the feeling to ripen enough for it to express itself almost entirely on its own), or deliberate activity (through some as-yet undiscovered mental operation or technical ruse that would attune me to it, in other words, chasing after it instead of letting it come to me). But if I were to conclude that it would be better not to take action before I am sure it would be wise to do so, not to embark upon one path or another without being fully prepared, my intent to wait so as not to spoil anything by too precipitous an approach would be derailed by my perpetual haste. When I am not writing, I actually experience a sickness I believe is comparable to what, for the junkie, is the state of withdrawal—in this case, being deprived of the drug that is the quest for poetry (as passionate an affair as that of the gambler consumed by the game that will lead to his fortune or ruin) and, condemned to a void that can't be filled by a reading or performance created by someone else, I suffer a sort of asphyxia, the victim of poisoned breaths that consume an interior space where nothing exists to resist them. Certainly, wisdom will sometimes command me to wait until the moment I can sense the fruit is just about to fall. But can I bear to live in such inaction and not rush to try my luck, even if afterwards I have some regrets: for mishandling something that deserved eloquence and having forever changed, damaged it; or for having, on the contrary, said something too elegantly that hadn't deserved mention and that illuminated nothing for myself or for anyone else; or, swinging between these two poles, for having written badly about something pointless and all because, to put an end to my suffering, I felt the need to write something at all costs, and because my judgment was clouded by a gnawing desire to succeed.

To have ruined the material from which a diamond could have been formed (or so we thought) by being too eager, or to have ruined nothing, as nothing worthy of any attention had been at stake, but to have fallen into pseudo-virtuosity by wishing to take part in this nothing, or rather—an even worse folly— having violently thrown myself into a ridiculous fantasy and having been in some way stupefied by it, an illness that is just as difficult to get rid of as it was easy to contract—in short, waste, sentimentality, and awkwardness that are not only some of the forms that cover up failure, but will be felt as sins more than gaffes, even though, far from considering himself invested in a highly privileged mission, the writer considers literary activity to be only a game with a single player. For it will be with this game like many other games that have a moral dimension, not only in the sense that cheating is prohibited, that losing by having been too subtle or too obtuse brings shame upon the writer, puts him in the position of the accused even if he immediately destroys the original and expresses remorse, as much as an athlete who—having been improperly trained, chosen a bad strategy, or simply lost his nerve—botched his performance. Shame with no apparent reason, since, if he considers literature a space of inalienable freedom and wishes to be useless, even as he resists being only a useless dealer of ephemeral pleasures, the writer—as opposed to the athlete, who is often a flag-bearer—is practically the only person involved and, despite his unbelievable pride, knows that the world won't actually hold it against him if there is a ridiculous lack of proportion between the ambitions he had while writing and the finished product. And yet, frequent regret—it would be easy to analyze it—that in my case perhaps rests on this: having cheated by trying to realize, by artificial means, the authentic poetry that I haven't completely given up believing "creates itself". . . But no! Dredging up this old, more-than-questionable argument is certainly madness and, lured by an abstraction, ignores the furious remorse that mingles with my anxiety when I am not working or that keeps me obsessing over petty details: you lazy, good-for-nothing bum, you navel-gazer, you're letting the little time you have left slip through your fingers! Isn't wasting your life—out of carelessness, not doing or doing only by halves that which, rightly or wrongly, you feel called to do while practicing your craft—the most imbecilic crime, since the person who commits it is its primary victim and since this self-destructiveness, not even an overt act but a surrender to inertia, lacks the intensity of the *no* expressed by the radical mode of scuttling that is suicide in its true form?

Regret when I do bad work, regret when I don't work at all. What a source of regret writing is for me, a passion that has become the only one I feel allowed to yield to in any circumstance and through which I would even say that I *would like* to know that I am crazy enough and at the same time courageous enough not to be deterred by the most desperate situations or worst-case scenarios I might have to face personally—a passion, then, that I take on without the slightest regret and that causes me regret only when I observe that, in one way or another, I am not in tune with it (and, notably, that I don't answer to my old idea of the "real poet," *in which the poetic imagination tends to substitute itself for a completely different mode of thinking, and this under the least favorable and most tragic circumstances)!* Regret that has, in some sense, been deferred and is waiting to strike since, as if regretting not having captured me at the very start, it now arrives to torment me through an activity which, precisely, I thought I could devote myself to in good conscience, not treating it as a vocation, of course, but rather assigning it the free and irreducible character of a game—of a game in which death is never directly confronted and that is hence more perilous than Russian roulette, but that, even when it doesn't rise to the level of a serious concern, seems—if it responds to a profound need—noble enough to have license to practice it in the gravest of contexts (a natural disaster or the disappearance of a loved one, for example) without it being seen as an inappropriate frivolity. I will have, in short, retreated in order to advance, given that this will be the way in which I devote myself to the game, one that is extremely important to me even though its lack of measurable results, or the fact of my not devoting myself to it completely, will become a pattern of remorse.

Remorse, I say, as my thoughts turn without any further contemplation to the old Christian monk's *my fault, my most grievous fault.* . . But is it really a matter of remorse? Or isn't it, rather, that I am nauseated by a mixture of feelings that are actually fairly diverse? I wouldn't know how to disavow remorse, for I make too great of a case for writing not to reproach myself, as I have done to an extreme, when I have done bad work or not worked at all (a rigorism that is partnered by my contempt for the writer who makes concessions, even if he isn't cynically "commercial"). Also anxiety, which I had already been feeling and hoped to rid myself of by working, but which persists because, either bad or weak-willed, my work—or a desire that was too vague to have been fulfilled—wasn't strong enough to relieve it. Deception, since I had counted on work to be an anxiety-lifter, but either the machine hadn't worked correctly or hadn't even been turned on. Panic and fear, since it could be that this strategy (a drug perhaps, but not the kind whose dosage you can increase when it turns out to be ineffective) will henceforth be inadequate—irreducibly—for one of these two reasons: my present inability, having been diminished by age, to write any-thing *good enough*, supremely exciting enough, to produce a liberating effect; or the now-radical impossibility of liberating myself from an anxiety that has become too constant and too strong for it to succumb to any remedy. Shame—my wounded vanity—of only having written something mediocre, proving that ultimately I am nothing but a hack, or of having written nothing, which could be a sign that I am completely empty, or even on the verge of senility. Grief, finally, for feeling excluded from a paradise and embarrassment for that, because if I am so excluded, I must be unworthy and, according to my miserable impression of it, flawed at the very core—too insignificant, too common to be invited to the party—soiled by this original sin: of being myself, a more unpardonable sin than these occasional offenses—excessive impatience or its opposite, negligence, putting on airs out of vanity or bad faith, a sort of treason for which I am quickly punished, feeling strangely embarrassed by my horribly distorted voice—offenses I don't overlook (not by a long shot!), but that are venial sins compared to the mortal flaw of mediocrity that I often fear is the true cause of my failures.

But why be afraid of being unworthy in an area in which I'm accountable to no one? If I were a distraught lover, it would be natural that I fear the gaze of the Dulcinea in whose eyes I wouldn't want to prove unworthy. If I were devoted to a task on which futures other than my own depended, it would be natural for my inability to complete it successfully to make me anxious. If I were paid for my work, I might worry—basic professional conscience—that I wouldn't perform as I should and would then be overpaid. Engaging in language in any respect, I have every right to be anxious, for I perhaps play too fast and loose with it and am not completely sure that it will hold. And yet, I know this irritating conviction by experience and return to it: the sense that I am the guilty party (as much as if I had floundered horribly through a delicate situation, sinned against good taste, made a serious gaffe, foolishly missed an opportunity, all things we often wring our hands over) grips me when I don't write or when I think that I am writing badly, that publishing the awful thing would certainly expose me to the cruelest of verdicts—What a loser! Who does he think he is? He's completely worthless!—without charging me with any crime, unless I am criticized for not having found either in words or things their required complicity and for having thrown myself into a world that, when I sought to communicate with it, remained as deaf as a post. If, however, I condemn myself without admitting these extenuating circumstances, isn't it because I implicitly recognize that I am directly in question, because writing or not writing, writing well or writing badly are not things that come from the outside like a gift I do or do not receive, but relate exclusively to myself, who is either capable or incapable of treating words and things with the discernment required to extract from them their poetic metal? An eye keen enough to capture the invisible, and a mind strong enough to exploit that capture (a matter of perception and then of putting into words, even though words may come first and assemble themselves less as a translation than a creation of something new), these are the required conditions in the end, not the negativism expressed by a purely blissful or aggravated state of waiting.

I must then eliminate once and for all my old tendency to look in every direction for some regenerative collaboration and childishly ask either my random working material or my instrument, language, for help that is as providential as the help wished for by the true believer who counts on a spontaneous flow of grace and, what's more, works to obtain it through prayer. I haven't the right to incriminate the path, the stream, the leaf, the pebble, or any living thing that is caught in the net of my awareness (be it even for a brief moment) any more than I do the urban landscape or the objects of various orders that inhabit my bedroom or any other room in whose atmosphere I am steeped, the words that have only an impalpable existence even less, not even the stagnation or agitation that my consciousness returns to explore if I don't work or if my work does not succeed: instead of washing my hands of this mishap as if powers distinct from my own had been at work, I bitterly reproach myself, my otherwise senseless remorse proving that I consider myself the number one person responsible, aware that in the case of deficiency or of failure, the onus is on me. On the one who, once his work is printed, shamelessly signs it, admitting that—however it may be received and however he may profit or suffer as a result—he had been its architect.

◇

Trees so high, so straight and so close together that inside them not a sound is heard, as if they had placed sound outside of our reach while soaring—fearless—towards the sky and pushing sound up, out of the compact mass of the highest branches, towards a space of quarantine.

. . . Or—on the horizontal and not the vertical—the mask (one might say) of silence that the sight of a tall, dense forest affixes to us, believing it is sleeping standing up, disoriented by that absence of sound that seems to prove an organ that is eye and not ear.

In 1918, I think, and with the hostilities not yet over, the explosion of the gunpowder factory in La Courneuve.

In Passy, in the Lamartine square, I am about to cross the threshold of the courtyard of Kaiser-Charavay, the conservative institution where, in high school, I was a student. The din is so loud that for a moment I have the impression, not of having heard a massive detonation, but of having received a heavy blow to the head. Did feeling take the wrong door? My muscles seem to have reacted before I even heard the sound.

After the explosion, a cascade of broken glass, and this time it was via the tympanum—incontestably—that I was informed. A devil who disappears as quickly as he emerged from his box, a shopkeeper on the avenue Victor Hugo leaps from his shop, quickly lowers the metal shutters and, with the dexterity of a mouse vanishing into his hole, goes back inside somehow. Maybe through some kind of cat flap hidden in the shutters? (But only "maybe," since I doubt in retrospect that such a hatch existed.)

◇

Warm light.
Cool touch.

Sloppy kiss.
Crashing cymbal.

Soft contours.
Hard liquor.

Flat melody.
Brilliant harmony.

Spicy dish.
Bland arrangement.

Boring view.
Charming painting.

Rough tastes.
Soft music.

Harsh talk.
Brilliant acoustics.

Shrill tone.
Velvet voice.

Sour puss.
Syrupy song.

◇

The colza whose yellow irritates the teeth and that is more of a lemon than an oil. . .

Innumerable are the things that do not resemble what they actually are (a leaf, for example, that nothing reveals to be a lung, an airplane that is arguably too heavy to imitate a bird, a computer that doesn't appear to be a brain) and numerous are those with a deceptive appearance (the bear who seems meek, the serpent coiled on the ground, the fish whose gills are not ears, the moon's disc suspended on high, the phantom tree, the dead man sleeping).

Not muddying the waters but cutting to the quick, not beating around the bush but grabbing equivocation by the horns or slicing through it like a Gordian knot, that is perhaps the A B C of poetry.

The capricious acolyte that is the cat, more of a companion to the black servant than to Olympia. Mustn't the scene have its witness, just as the painting has its audience? But nothing in this scene, centered around a courtesan who places her sex between parentheses with a nonchalant hand, seems to concern the feline, and we wonder to what end, if he isn't limited to seeking out a corner of the bed where he can sleep peacefully, he will make the round of inspection for which he seems to be preparing himself. Besides, it doesn't matter what his large, open eyes are looking at and which, deprived of speech, he wouldn't be able to share with us, the ones who are looking. What counts—to someone for whom this image of high chivalry from nearly a century ago inspires reverie—is that this familiar spirit or diabolical sidekick is there, entitled, needing neither an invitation nor a justification for his presence, and that his tail (another ribbon the color of ink) rises up and flutters as if to express expectancy by tracing a question mark.

◇

THE AVENUE, that in our imagination is damp, dilapidated, covered in leaves, and that often promises and turns out to be so empty between its faded gardens and blind walls that, when its gates are unlocked, they open with pillowed sounds, like a bare-foot walk across a floorboard firm enough so that not even the slightest creak issues from it.

And yet, especially in cities, many avenues are nothing like those sober but appealing boulevards that, dampening rumor and undoing its venomous power, serve as havens from the villainy of the modern world. Our old-fashioned daydreams are contradicted, for example, by the Champs-Elysées, whose name lies twice: a wide road, almost still-new, where from morning until night the roar of comings and goings violates the peace that the word "avenue" seems to claim as a virtue, as well as the vaporous fields haunted by souls of the dead whose past adventures and fortunes are now nothing more than recollections made in vain.

◇

Heart with twin handles: which side do we choose?
Diamond not stable or square, standing on one of its points.
Club forged by the hands of a dexterous blacksmith.
Spade that bleeds black.

◇

Black with red markings and pointed beaks, two small birds escort me, flying several feet ahead (at times closer, at times further away, and occasionally parting from one another) on the trail I am following, holding my dog on a leash. One of them, sometimes, perches on a stone, while the other flutters about in the hollow of a tree where his batting wings seem to be the only thing keeping him from being engulfed by it. An alimentary quest, a search for insects or other animalcules—a zigzagging chase that the dog, too busy sniffing around in the grass, ignores —was the likely reason for this this low flight, perhaps an early warning sign of even more bad weather that, hearing me gush about how beautiful the morning was, the owner of the field I was passing through predicted for three days from now, based on the wind's direction (blowing from the northeast) and the fact that this year, 1978 (whose month of May is ingloriously approaching), is likely to be bad, since it has thirteen moons.

I vaguely wonder (without taking the idea very seriously) if, following only my whim, I should pursue these two birds— guides, messengers, emissaries from what jurisdiction and to what end?—to see what they have to show me; or if I should abandon their euphoric pageantry . . . But after around a quarter of an hour, or not even that, I lose sight of them: no longer ahead of me, they have flown towards the right side of the path and so I can no longer make them out, not because they are too far away, I think, but because they blend in, tone on tone, with the color of the tilled and freshly seeded soil.

I am not unhappy with the way this matter was resolved. I would have felt a sort of shame if I had decided to abandon my friendly pair of scouts at the moment—probable—when to continue following behind this winged couple would have taken me so far off course that after my quasi-solitary walk, I would have returned home late for lunch with the woman I paired up with so many moons ago—so many I can hardly believe it.

$\diamond$

On summer vacation in an establishment that's part-hotel, part-sanatorium in the Black Forest: 700 meters above sea level and 15 kilometers away from Baden-Baden (whose name corresponds to "Bains-les-Bains," near the Vittel and Contrexéville Vosges), "Bühlerhöhe" ("Hauts-de-Bühl" or "Bühl-le-Haut"), the counterpart to Bühlertal or "Bühl-le-Val," which neighbors a small commercial village christened Bühl, full stop. Essentially, Bühlerhöhe—where in earlier times one had to suffer the miserable weather that affected that part of Europe—isn't much more than a crossroads, near as the crow flies to Baden-Baden but connected to that station of antiquated luxury by a road full of hairpin turns, highly unsuitable for speeding and assuming, when riding the bus to go there, the scale of a small adventure on a road that, if traveled on foot, would be no problem at all for a walker who was even the slightest bit accustomed to mountain trails.

The Black Forest is usually well-named, for its woods are bleak, but during those few rainy days it should have been called the Gray Forest, thickly veiled as it was by rain and fog, apart from some short periods of sun that were of course too brief and that we were too quickly inclined to forget had kept us from becoming completely mired in the gloom. A forest no longer haunted by brigands and gnomes, and that in those dark days also seemed to have been deserted by its feathered and furry creatures, but in foul as much as fair weather the trees continued to impose, particularly when, seeing them fallen and stripped of their bark in piles by the side of the road, it was easier to evaluate how tall those yellow and often odoriferous boles actually were. A dense forest that was only intermittently spoiled by a flood of tourists, and where anyone repelled by an excess of human density could still, without straying too far, find himself feeling completely isolated, as long as he wasn't returned to the loathsome contingencies of the present day by the strident passing of a military plane.

I climbed Baden-Baden again that afternoon, not on foot but in a car we had rented to transport our familial group, under a sky so cloudy that the sun seemed to struggle to pierce through it in places, in very pale rays. At a curve in the road high up enough so that a broad landscape fanned out below it, or rather, gave just a glimpse of itself behind a misty screen, the light of the sun that almost seemed as if it were already gone, even though night was nowhere near close to falling, resurrected itself in an unexpected way: two or three vast pools of clear light on the blur of the landscape, on the lowland side, lactescent patches that spread out with no clear relation to the structure of the plot of land (a bit like the way color and line are systematically disassociated in certain modern paintings) and partially engulfed, irrespective of their contours, bunches of trees and groups of houses that seemed no bigger than toys. Patches we could call *substantial*, like the way, on a smaller scale, a greasy or sugary thing may stain a piece of fabric, that seemed to reveal the materiality of the light (to show the thing that illuminates rather than the things that appear under a certain kind of illumination). Limpid patches somehow transforming the terrestrial landscape into a kind of negative of the celestial landscape, which itself was stained by fat, dark clouds.

Instantly, I had the impression that I should follow the revelation taking place before my eyes to the letter, that I would
find a crucial truth about the world and my destiny in this
landscape that was both clouded over and in sun, that both
above and below seemed to illustrate the Manichean antago-
nism of two principles and whose terrestrial half, an inverted
replica of the celestial half, would have been—at ground
level—its translation in the language spoken by the things
that, as palpable bodies rather than castles in the air, form our
habitual surroundings. A glorious truth expressing a glorious
spectacle that seemed to have been arranged to bring me a
kind of salvation—life rehabilitated—by showing me that
light exists as well as shadow, or better yet: by making me a
witness to its triumph over obscurity, a patent triumph, since
the way in which it superimposed itself on the details of our
world (accidents of terrain, vegetation and typically human
arrangements of clusters of houses) affirmed its transcendence.
A dazzling image, elevating to a sublime level—that of the
world as it should be—the nauseating swing of the pendulum
(hope/despair, pleasure/suffering, passion/disgust) imposed on
us by our personal lives and our roles as witnesses or even
actors in a History that alternates chivalrous advances with
falls into the horrors of war. This sight, as moving as a vision,
probably suggested this kind of idea to me because it stirred up
an old religious quandary. I might have even called it the mani-
festation of a positively divine light, if the word "God" had any
place in my vocabulary. But I do not like that a stand-in,
catch-all word whose idol-with-feet-of-clay angle only makes
me want to shrink from it (because of my anti-Himalaya bent
that also deters me from masterpieces that are discussed only
in hushed tones, like the disciples of Wagnerism did in their
day). Rather than call upon a notion that is too enormous not
to be hollow, I prefer—returning to the present—to align

myself with the nothing that, without seeming like nothing, makes everything turn joyful, the moment we remember and whose memory, if it stays fresh enough, will endure, for it proves that something other than ugliness exists—like the meteorologic conditions that, for a moment, instilled a sense of plentitude in me through a play of transparence and opacity that, although I appreciated their powers of illusion, I was aware—deeply aware—signified nothing.

That this play of light differed from a perceptible path of light (a ray of a projector, for example) and that it took the form of patches falling on a landscape seen from far away and on high instead of a floor or pieces of furniture, was essential. For its contemplation to take a quasi-metaphysical turn, it had to surpass the restricted environment of the laboratory and affect an ample enough slice of nature to inspire reflection on the universal. And it also had to be something other than a beam of light, just as how, at a certain altitude, cloudy skies can sometimes seem very beautiful. Light in puddles, in patches, comparable to pools attesting to a flood, that's what allowed it, eternally majestic and yet within our reach, to act so powerfully upon the imagination. But did it need such a noble adjuvant to flourish? An experience of a lesser, but perhaps even more surprising, flash of light, which occurred directly before the one I have just attempted to relate (with limited success, I can say without false modesty, knowing that anything I could say would fall short of that illumination) seems, in its very secularity, to prove the opposite, and to show that very little, in fact, is needed to make that leap.

The night of our arrival at Bühlerhöhe, in the dining room whose crown mouldings on the ceiling first made me think of the 18th century, when in actuality the sanatorium was constructed around 1930, I was sitting in front of a placard that was entirely covered by a large color photograph whose subject, unappealing in itself, was a logging site reproduced life-size, as they say: behind the pink heather in the foreground and towards the center of a clearing that probably had nothing to do with the Black Forest, or at least with its standard characteristics, since the trees surrounding it were not pines, and some birches (if I am identifying them correctly) figured among them, a bend in the river was met in the top half of the photo by an almost spherical bower formed by the foliage that reached up to the tops of the high trees. With my back to the window, I couldn't see the sunset—and it was hidden anyway by a lowered blind—but only, on the photograph, the luminous bars stemming from the rays that, piercing through the slats, struck it in such a way that the crests of the water seemed to sparkle. Furthermore, to the left and the right of the image, one at the foot of a fairly large tree, the other planted, it seemed, in the heather, two identical wall lamps with lit bulbs—actual elements of the dining room's lighting system—appeared to belong to this imitation landscape and played (immediately I thought of this famous work that I had been introduced to by a scale model, although it was a poor substitute) a role analogous to the lamp held by the woman in the unsettling diorama, half relief, half *trompe-l'oeil*, in which Marcel Duchamp presents, in a banal landscape that includes a shining waterfall an outstretched naked woman whose head and feet are not shown and whose most apparent function is to carry a lamp that is actually lit, while other elements of the work, whatever function they serve, are only counterfeit. Juxtapostion of authentic reality (the lamp) and false reality, just as how in the Bühlerhöhe sanatorium the actual lamps producing electric light participated in a simulated landscape that was struck by natural light (less intense than the other but in some way more *real*) of the sunset passing through the blinds, a complex combination in which several orders of confluence intertwined—light and shadow, given thing and fabricated thing, real and unreal—and a singular ambiguity cast a powerful spell. . . But isn't what we call "poetry," an emotion that the mind constructs as much as it receives, almost exactly a spell of this kind, the bastard child of a conjugation of shadow and light and a marriage of spontaneity and artifice, on the borderline of deception and truth? To fix moments of disturbance in which everything seems to be called into question and try to give them a second wind, or else counter their infrequency through equivalents procured entirely through fabrication, that is one of the essential goals of poetry in its written form.

A light that, in the actual landscape as much as the photographed one, acted as an overlay and produced a phantasmagoria, with its unpredictable shadows whose formless design made them more evocative than if they had been geometrical, that is what appeared to me, not to teach me something about my destiny or the ways of the universe but to shed—by chance, and as if by a vocation inherent to its nature—a bit of light on poetry. To make me understand that, since it originates from a conjunction or an amalgamation of heterogeneous terms, it can only be a hybrid—siren, centaur, griffon?—that moves in the equivocal. To lead me to conclude that for it to cast the spell that fulfills us, it need not hold an eloquent or profound conversation, only abruptly announce that *it is there*, superimposed upon but integrated within what exists, and not alongside of it. To provide me with a connecting thread by showing me that regardless of its content, and whatever form it may take, it is not a flight from real life or traffic with another world but something that touches upon, so to speak, the *surreal*, something that concretizes—in a way that oddly intersects with etymology—the effect of luminous stigmata that superimpose themselves on the reality, thus transfigured, of a landscape, or on the fictional reality of the photograph of a place.

Owing to my clumsiness while wielding knife and fork, the patches of light that had led me to daydream so intensely during my stay at Bühlerhöhe spilled over, in the form of tomato sauce, without hitting my pants, onto the lapel of my jacket during my final meal in that sanatorium where, surrounded by other creatures (often none too spry) who were lured at times by the dining room, at times by the lounge, at times by the terrace, three or four specters of the male sex—not all of whom were my elders, I sadly discovered—were circulating, walking with slow, small steps, almost as if they were *Noh* performers, pressing down on their canes with rubberized tips (as opposed to the steel tips of the martial accessories used by many alpine hikers). The oldest phantom, three years older than my wheelchair-bound relative whom my wife and I, hardly agile ourselves, were accompanying, was assisted by his English sister who was barely more robust than he and by a young nurse they had brought with them from Paris, followed by another figure: a tall and brittle Dutch woman of 95 who, flanked by a traveling companion who listened patiently during her lengthy monologues, got around with the aid of a kind of mobile balustrade made of steel tubes that she held on to with both hands each time she placed her healthier left foot in front of her gnarled right, a Semiramis who carried with her, like a piece of a stage set, the symbolic fragment of a rampart that she only stowed away when she sat down.

Despite their beautiful red color, I accorded no poetic value to the constellation of spots with which, on the eve of leaving the Black Forest, I soiled my outfit, the brand-new houndstooth coat that, after the morning's medical business and my afternoon walk, I usually put on for the relative formality of dinner. A piece of clothing whose loss, if it couldn't have been cleaned, would have irritated me all the more because it was probably the last coat I would have ordered for myself, since I owned enough jackets even without that one to last me until my death—which I shamefully hope takes place before my companion's, whose absence I can't imagine enduring—as long as it isn't later than I expect, an order with the color of an adieu for the preoccupied snob and unquiet man I have always been.

◇

Rainy forest not of rain but trees like fine-toothed combs.
Pool of mica.
Fog the color of oblivion.
Snow that my dog licks as if it were an ice cream cone.

$\diamond$

Having just entered (we assume) the bedroom that seems to be lit solely by the naked body of the lady of the house, what keeps the devoted servant, no longer sweltering in the tropics, from splitting apart her voluminous bouquet and scattering across Olympia's body the petals that—flower-on-flower instead of tone-on-tone—would highlight the paleness of her skin and at the same time sharpen its perfume?

◇

The pasture, the forest, or the river whose view brings us peace, and the thought that the Nature into which we are born and die is not only something that cities hide behind sometimes sordid disguises, but also this, something into which it wouldn't seem so terrible to disappear.

Probably because they are too powerful, neither the sea nor the mountains communicate such peace to me, suggesting that I create, with gentleness, a relation of intimacy between myself and the exterior.

◇

Billiard ball removed from the break shot, incandescent cannonball, shining medallion highlighted by a translucent complexion, crystal ball of the seer that captivates our eye: at the center of a pearl-gray sky in a Chinese or Japanese painting, the setting sun below tapered trees too dark to be green and that, in the foreground, trigger an increasingly clear spacing out of hill-sides eventually drowning in a Rhineland plain that no visible horizon line can enclose.

◇

To the left of the road, on a piece of tilled earth, I discover gossamer threads languorously stretching from crest to crest that shimmer in the sprawling light. Slightly higher up, here and there, a capricious blizzard of black dots: gnats whose flight, accompanied by no buzzing, doesn't seem numbed by the cold.

The cake whose oversize slices were served to me by an invisible plow (or one of its avatars in our ridiculously industrialized era) seemed even more giant since I had lost all sense of its actual size at the sight of the delicate rigging of spun sugar—the arachnean shimmer that had so surprised me from just a short distance away—that connected, by skipping over some of them, the more or less angular clumps that were uncoordinated by any real geometry.

Fat, nauseating pieces that I might find as appetizing as slices of mocha cake if I didn't know them to be so coarse and stuffed with foreign bodies that they would make an atrocious squeal when chewed by whomever yielded to the urge to sample a taste. . .

◇

Star with branches too spiky
*   to gaze at safely.*
Blue sky to drown in.
Night whose dawn struggles to scrub itself clean.
Sun that's visible only when one is ill.
Moon, empty plate or silent gong.

◇

It's not with the four seasons—a hamster wheel over which current events have no control—that the naked Olympia must reconcile me. I understand all too well that nature, a nonhuman theatre of constant renewal, is the environment to which I am biologically destined to return, and it matters little whether or not I resign myself to that fact. What this figure (neither a nymph nor a rustic bather but a woman resting on a bed) instead reminds me of, by the intervention of her jewelry and other secular accessories, is that, just like fashion, life takes its course—not in an immutable cycle, but according to a forward-moving, linear progression of before, during, and after—and that, affecting us directly and hence with some importance even though on the superhuman level of cosmic vastness its dimensions are miniscule, History exists.

I try to locate myself in relation to this History, a parade of fleeting and sequential episodes that parallel those of my life, and I would like to integrate with it, if possible—at least through my work, a lifeless construction if it isn't expressly topical—my own impermanence. If my work is based on dateless contemplation (vegetative, in some way), how can I pronounce the words I would now like to pronounce that would return to the sensibility of our era something greater than what I have taken from it? The *presence* of that urbanite,

Manet's Olympia, urges me by her modernity (intensity, proximity, immediacy) not to doze off into static, vain contemplation.

◇

Enribbon,
encircle,
enclose,
embed,
enroot,
insert,
enrich,
illumine,
enlighten,
inflame,
inseminate.

◇

What circus isn't the most beautiful thing in the world—the world and its beauties shown in all its beauty?

The circus—where misfortune, if it exists, is not on the bill—offers a *glorious* vision of the world: the triumph of man over animals and over his own body, which scoffs at constraints like gravity while intelligence, which makes him the king of creation, knows how to thwart causality, as the illusionist's thaumaturgy proves.

Animals who have been taught clever tricks (monkeys, dogs, seals), others who have been tamed (elephants on parade, the trunk of one gently holding the tail of another and deftly maneuvering masses that seem freshly detached from the telluric crust, spirited horses who are nevertheless obedient, decorated, braided, and so tightly bridled that their mouths almost touch their chests), others still who are dominated either gently or by force behind quickly-arranged metal grates (lions, tigers, and less imposing but equally dangerous beasts who have been reduced, barring accident, to innocuousness).

All the marvels of the world—or those that can be assembled—enclosed in a circular space with a narrow perimeter. Harmony, accord, a "concert" of nations that reunite to fly their flags and celebrate one another. The human comedy, illustrated in debonair fashion by foolish Auguste, who makes a mockery of the shrewd, brilliant clown. The promises of evolution kept by those who walk or ride the unicycle upside down, improving upon the upright position that followed walking on all fours so many moons ago. The thrilling promotions of the small circuses of yesteryear: the usherette who turns out to be an equilibrist and the cashier a serpent charmer.

On sawdust or brush carpet, the sublime art is in the rendez-vous itself: in poses like those the men of bronze took (a race of carnies with metallic skin which, I think, is now extinct), marmoreal beings sing a hymn to the splendor of the unique structure of our species.

Fun for everyone (adults as much as children), the circus—rich or poor—is also a beautiful lesson, since the modest or sumptuous range of its beauties makes visible, even to those who will never believe in terrestrial paradise, how beautiful it is to live in the world.

Towards the end of the summer of 1957, at the Champ-de-Mars in Florence, a stratospheric grand finale crowned Circus Togni's performance: emerging from a perfume vaporizer, fluffy clouds of steam covered the entire ring, under a starry sky that the roof of the canvas tent had become through a play of luminous projections. Girls, clowns, dwarves, all of the artists were there, including a trio (a woman and two men as scantily clad as ancient statues) who minutes earlier, at the center of a circle of water jets, imitated figures from a Bernini-style fountain.

Ten years later, near the Hilton hotel in Berlin, the entrance of the Sarrasini circus seemed, at night, as if it were at the end of a long avenue bordered by a double bank of electric lamps: a *trompe-l'oeil* owing to a perspectival effect created by converging lines of lamps focused on a huge panel behind the doorway, an immeasurable, dreamlike correspondence.

Oversensitive to pain, if it's not sybaritic, and distressed by medical exams focusing on organs located below the waist that, actual low blows, involve the insertion of a tubular instrument into the antrum or narrow pass to be explored, I demanded—braving the taunts of the doctor who had prescribed the tests that the vesical trouble I was suffering from required—full anesthesia, even though a local anesthetic is common practice in such a case. In my defense, I will say that another practitioner, our family doctor who considered the thing to be quite painful from personal experience, encouraged me to make this demand, insisting on it all the more because, unlike his colleague, he knew me well!

Rather than being knocked unconscious by the injection as soon as it was given to me, I felt myself—contrary to my expectations—slide gradually into unconsciousness, which surprised me a little afterwards. When I woke up, while coming out of the blank spell caused by the anesthetic, a strange feeling came over me that didn't disappear right away and which I shared in confidence first with the family doctor who was kind enough to escort me, and then again with both him and my wife in the room where I am now, the little room I'm staying in at the Victor-Massé clinic near Pigalle and the clubs I used to frequent in the days when, as a single man, I used to roam the streets at night: my head was spinning terribly and I had an abominable case of cotton mouth.

After several minutes of gradually coming to my senses, I realized what was actually going on: I wasn't drunk at all but under the effect, not yet entirely dissipated, of the anesthetic, and I was mistakenly under the impression that I had attended a wild party during which I drank so much that I had passed out.

When I returned to myself completely, I thought I could trace this illusion back to its probable source. Hadn't I noticed the lighting fixture in the operating room, a large disc literally plastered with electric projectors aimed at my body laid out underneath? So it must have been this strong light coming from above, and the fact of being surrounded by various people gathered together as if for an *Anatomy Lesson* (my usual doctor, his fellow surgeon who conducted the operation, the anesthesiologist, and a nurse) that caused me to imagine—in a kind of very brief dream—that, drunk as a skunk, I was at the center of a crowd in a room as brightly lit as the expression *a giorno* suggests, a boisterous celebration supervised by a chandelier.

Could we hope to be blessed with such a vision at the moment of death? That's the ending—a dubious but rather reassuring one—that I gave, the day after this sort of adventure reduced to a flash that didn't even, strictly speaking, qualify as a scene, to the account I managed to make of it. Today, seven years have passed, and a memory returns to me: the other doctor, the one who considered full anesthesia excessive, had tried to encourage me by telling me about a patient of his who had recently endured the ordeal himself and considered it very manageable, crudely adding that obviously it was nothing like "spending the night with a dancer." Combined with what was perhaps a bit of shame about having shown myself to be overly pusillanimous, had this idea of a sexcapade with a a ballerina hovered over me when, emerging from a sleep that, while it anesthetized me, certainly didn't submerge me in complete darkness, I created a memory of scandalous drunkenness in the brouhaha of a party under a chandelier worthy of an Opéra cupola?

◇

Falling and spreading down to her hips, hidden by the back-rest on her seat, the beautiful flaxen hair of the female driver, not of a farmer's tractor but the bus I take almost every day. While getting on at the front as usual and flashing the card with my photograph on it, I saw her face, coarse even though its features were symmetrical and sharp—a face I continued to resculpt in my mind, purging it of its flaws when, sitting some distance away, I saw her impressive mane again. It didn't seem as if the other passengers—or most of them—admired her as much as I did . . . But in truth, I'll never know: my own face probably didn't express what I was feeling and it's possible the same went for theirs. Still, I'd bet that none of these strangers felt as much pleasure as I did in knowing I was being piloted by this vigorous and quiet Amazon, admiring her haughty look and the quasi-divine shamelessness with which, perched on a higher seat than those of the commoners the vehicle was carrying, she displayed the flowing, long blond hair that contrasted with the somber, conspicuously less silken gray of her vest.

◇

Absent: the intimate muff concealed by the fanned-out hand that Olympia places firmly on her thigh—for the artist, a compromise (one might say) between his desire for realism and the customs of the era that, in painting, deemed hairy female genitals taboo—seems to find, at the cost of a lightning bolt, a substitute in two other compositional elements: the lushness of the bouquet brought by the turbanned servant and the blackness of the cat prowling around for God knows what.

Another such flash, we may well imagine: at her left ear, the trinket whose rose and floral folds evoke the organ that we may assume is adorned or made savage by the muff that is just as invisible.

◇

    I go back up the rue de l'Éperon to pick some money up from the post office. In the middle of the street, I see a middle-aged woman, poorly but not too shabbily dressed, who's panhandling. More virago than rag-picker, she begs in a weeping tone, adding—an argument that must seem convincing to her—that she isn't, after all, a thief. Her whining, obviously an act, annoys me and there is something about her entire being that disgusts me. And so, I give her nothing and continue, without stopping, on my way.

    Almost immediately, in a reaction that arises while I'm waiting at the postal check window, I reproach myself for this first reaction and tell myself that if I'm coming out of the post office loaded with cash, I can't in good conscience—unless I take a different route out of shame—refuse the beggar a little something if I see her again.

    I do in fact find her, wrapped up in the same tattered coat of heavy brown and beige fabric, but now standing on the sidewalk, almost leaning against the wall, and no longer in the street, where nothing in fact would interrupt her but the occasional vehicle.

    When, after receiving the franc and three 20 centimes coins—a little extra to sweep away my remorse—that I deposit in her open and outstretched wallet, she thanks me with a large and amiable smile and then, in an unctuous voice that's completely different from the one she used several minutes ago, wishes me a "good day" (which I ought to accept, since in actual fact my days are far from being excellent), she disgusts me even more than before and I reproach myself for having performed, not out of the kindness of my heart but out of a stupid fear of being judged, what is commonly seen as a charitable gesture.

◇

I no longer see the discrete, blackish mass of a miniature bulldog who, almost every time I walked down the rue Grégoire-de-Tours, a narrow alley well-suited to its Merovingian name, used to sit there like a protective spirit. Never too spry to begin with and (I suppose) now very old, he has probably died.

Out of fear, most likely of being ridiculed for visibly demonstrating the sentimentality of a grandmother towards the canine species, I never once petted that animal who was so small that in order to do so I would have had to conspicuously stoop down. But I was always happy to see him, whether he stood motionless in front of a door (his, I imagine), or strolled about with a measured, disillusioned gait, or exchanged, without ever becoming too agitated, some friendly greetings with one of his fellows of his or another breed.

I could call him a tranquil monster guardian, tutelary spirit, or household deity without exaggeration, for it would be difficult for me to otherwise express the measure of the feeling of peace that each one of our encounters, two feet away from my house, gave me, and that kept me from returning home with a face as sullen as that animal whose sad eyes and flattened snout appeared to take on all of the moroseness that it silently reflected.

◇

His annoyance with growing old making him cantankerous, and his cantankerousness amplifying his irritation, was something worse than a vicious cycle: when his bad mood began to escalate, no one could predict what heights it would reach. . .

(I'm ashamed to have come to this, which is why I distance myself from the thing by containing it in the third person and, another interval, in the imperfect tense, like a schoolmaster exiling to the far edges of the classroom the young student who behaves so badly that it is only right that he be put in the corner.)

◇

—*One day, I found that the circle around me had grown so small that I had become a stylite, without ever intending it!*

—*On a marble column?*

—*More like melting wax, as the circle had been. A stylite, then, on a candle: a candle for whom I am the burning flame.*

◇

If, writing not out of caprice, material interest or thirst for glory but to defend against the idea of death, I see my writing as a fragile carapace I build for myself with words I find ready-made and use to the best of my ability (words whose alignment on the page reproduces the sinuous and intermittent itinerary that my hand, armed with a pen, traces with rejections, breaks, and retouches in a labyrinth I move through with cautious steps, as if, doubting my lamplight, I were waiting for the pen to guide me, leading me by the hand), I would logically like to inhabit these writings, or else they would be only empty shells, not pieces of an armament but a broken panoply whose elements I leave scattered around me as if I were a child at play. But what's the point of writing—choosing phrases, each of which, in its linear progression, is simultaneously the tightrope I must walk, the cable I hold on to, and the horizon I fix my eyes on—if only to create a diversion, avoid confrontation, and hence resolve nothing! All the same, I certainly do have various ways of inhabiting my writing, and it would be shortsighted to think that confession or autobiography are the only appropriate ones. What's more, relics are not the only kinds of talismans, and I don't see why in that respect the thing I draw from memory should take precedence over the thing I imagine. What counts is only that this thing, whose character hardly matters, resembles me (in the way that a painted or drawn portrait, even one that isn't allusive, may be closer to the original than a photograph) and that, even if it is purely a fiction that relates to me only very loosely, it reveals my most significant traits and, because of that, reveals me.

For all of this not to be simply a game of metaphors that seduces me while proving to be nothing more than a play on words, it would be necessary, through writing, with the obstinacy of a mole digging out his tunnel, to create a simulacrum that, when my anxiety attaches itself to it, qualifies as protective armor: not necessarily a mold cast on the spot but an outfit that, both tailored to my body and endowed with its own form, would constitute an essential part of the visible reality in which I am seen through the eyes of others as well as to my own, I who—normally—present myself as clothed rather than laying myself bare. Certainly, this is not a matter of dressing up, or even less of disguising, the thoughts that I can only relieve myself of by revealing them, but of dressing them in a way that is vibrant and exact enough for them, once released into the open air, to establish themselves without giving rise to the equivocal. A major question for me since, doing so, I clothe myself in an envelope that, by externalizing me and becoming my way of existing in the minds of strangers, allows me to stretch the limits of my mortal self.

◇

Orpheus and his lyre.
Homer and his white cane.
Dante and the hood that distinguishes him from Virgil.
Ronsard and his crown of laurels.
Cyrano and his legendary nose.
Racine and his curly wig.
Buffon and his lace gloves.
Voltaire in his Voltaire chair.
Mirabeau's pockmarked face.
Balzac and his nightgown.
Gautier and his red doublet.
Mallarmé under his plaid.
Rimbaud dressed more like a convict than a smuggler.
Tolstoy in his peasant shirt.
Wilde in lilies that soon turn to nettles.
Jarry in bicycle shorts.
Max Jacob wearing a yellow star.
Roussel aboard his roulotte.
Apollinaire with a bandaged head.
Joyce and his thick glasses.
Kafka topped by a Magrittian bowler.

◇

CHOIR, *gleefully chanting in full voice, while the hall fills up:*

S'il te ceinture,	If he corners you,
fais gaffe au satyre Larigot:	watch out for Larigot the lecher:
en sa sainte ire	he's a holy terror
il t'agrafera le haricot!	he'll drive you mad!

From the arches, a sign descends bearing two words, printed in large type and followed by one or several exclamation points, that we may assume constitute the title of the play:

BUT NO!

Then come three knocks, spaced out and sharply articulated.
Nothing happens.
The three knocks are repeated several times, louder and louder and faster and faster until they become continuous.
A long silence, then a single, very faint knock.

ACT I

The curtain rises on complete darkness.
MALE VOICE (*whining*): I'm cold. I'm hungry. I'm frightened. I'm bored. . .

The stage lights gradually fade up, revealing a vast, desert prairie with—stage right—a crisp top hat, pearl-gray with a black ribbon, hanging on a jagged-edged post.

The curtain slowly falls, accompanied by modulated whistling, as is done in the navy.

ACT II

The curtain rises on a lush forest where a light, continuous rustling of leaves can be heard.

THE SAME VOICE (*yelling*): Dinnertime! Dinnertime! (*A pause, and then in an aside*): But wartime, also wartime . . .

Then the deeply rhythmic sounds of marching troops, then the din of a jackhammer that remains audible after the curtain falls and, at the height of the crescendo, abruptly stops.

ACT III

The curtain rises on an enormous mirror that reflects the entire hall. At the back of the house and at its highest point (what used to be called "paradise" and has more recently been known as the "peanut gallery"), an invisible loudspeaker.

THE LOUDSPEAKER: (*in a nasal tone and decrescendo that fades into total silence*): Polly want a cracker? Polly want a cracker? (Etc.)

A gunshot close by, and the tumultuous fall of the curtain, as if it had become unhinged.

MUFFLED CHOIR, *barely audible, while the audience disperses:*

O Zigomar, O Zigoto,
will you one day pull the trigger
scared to death of the Grim reaper
He's bound to catch you, maybe later
but always all too soon?

◇

An actor with no dressing room for getting into costume before making his entrance and who, to make himself up, will have to wait until he's played a few more roles and becomes less green than when, cued by a useless stage manager, he appears from the wings. The play is improvised—sloppily improvised—and performed only once, in front of a crowd of people who are mostly thinking about their own affairs and who occasionally fidget and blanket the lines delivered onstage with their murmurs. As he senses that the curtain is about to fall, the actor's stage fright escalates, and soon this character who thinks he is the star of the show will find himself robbed for the second or third time of delivering what he would like to be the last line of the play, a line that, like his fellow players, he improvises while almost always resorting to pathetic clichés.

◇

Haunted by the prospect of the evil tricks that his life, already long, might play on him before he vanishes, he tried to come to terms with it. If his situation ever became too unbearable, he could at least escape it with the help of a lethal dose of sleeping pills. And he imagined these two scenarios in particular: if, distraught by widowerhood as if he were an orphan with no guardian, he felt destined to end his days in terrible suffering; if (a possibility that also worried him, although it nagged at him less severely) he found that his intelligence was deteriorating to such a degree that he would soon be considered a vegetable in the eyes of his family and friends. Still, when he steeled himself by thinking that if he were afflicted by one of these falls from grace, he could always administer a remedy to end it all, certain things eluded him.

First, it was his companion's presence—a presence that fortified and encouraged him—that would give him the courage to ready himself for an act that demanded it, even if it were executed painlessly or without bloodshed. So how could he rely on that remedy if, in order to have the guts to use it when the time came, he would need that wife who, obviously, would no longer be there?

And then, if his mind had seriously deteriorated, would he be lucid enough to notice? When the right moment to end it all arrived, would he know that the moment had come? And, if he were aware of his decline, wouldn't he have already become the object of too many humiliations to be able to redeem himself?

A less circumstantial, and perhaps most crippling delusion was that he could not see that suicide becomes more difficult at the point when, given one's advanced age, it would be most justified: at that stage, you have, luckily or unluckily, lost too much for your life to really be worth living, but at the same time, you have lost the necessary will—when the bell tolls—to draw the line.

It is likely that he will not draw—for lack of courage—that line that should be drawn, one way or another, when the bell tolls. . . And I know something about this, as "he" is only a mask that, speaking of something it would be more dignified to silence, I hid behind—but playfully, in plain sight, and as a matter of protocol rather than out of a desire to deceive.

◇

When old age frightens me, I sometimes try to console myself a little by telling myself that, if I haven't reached the heights I once dreamed of reaching, it would still be very wrong to remember my youth, if not as a Golden Age (something that childhood only is in the mind of an adult), at least as an era of greater purity than the ones that followed.

The prejudices, instilled in me almost as soon as I knew how to speak, that bound me to my social class, the bourgeoisie, and placed blinders on me that, despite the love for the poor that Christianity preaches, made me believe that my more affluent class was the only one worthy of consideration, had to be abolished, and in order to mitigate their effects, a long series of experiences accompanied by thorough reflection was necessary. Ill-equipped for rebellion, I had to wait until I was the daily user of a razor that was not my first, long after I had reached the stage following puberty to learn—hearing a friend, a great painter who was apparently incensed by the news that filled the papers, rail against the French decision to occupy the Ruhr like a creditor executing a foreclosure—that this country in which I was born, home of the storming of the Bastille and the battle of the Marne, could sometimes prove to be deplorable. For me, whose only ambition at the time was to soar to superhuman heights of the imagination, a power that I ingenuously attributed to poets with a furious desire to become one of their chosen few, this discovery was an important step: to glimpse that our number one enemy is not that universe whose laws of stone I sparred with using words, but the way in which we humans organize ourselves within it. And yet, I still hadn't learned—and it didn't happen right away—that it is ridiculous to condemn if we don't lift a finger to combat what appalls us. If I ended up "engaging myself" at all (even though that wasn't sanctioned by any contract), it wasn't only because circumstances drove me to it, but because I rejected this absurdity: cursing one's fate and constructing a second life in writing while doing nothing to rebuild the first. A matter, in short, less of passion than of logic.

It was only later on that I rid myself of the many ideas and attitudes that primarily allowed me to see myself in a particular light, for renouncing them ran counter to my deepest desires. Gradually, and with plenty of wavering, I threw overboard the beliefs that had only been held in place by the absence of any real test of them, joined with the seductive power they held over me. And as for my most deeply-rooted predilections, they too could not escape the reconsiderations that were based less on a concern for properly tending to my internal affairs than with my fundamental tendency towards doubt. And so, I was liberated from the sentiment, still imbued with religiosity, that had led me to conceive of art as a trap for transcendence rather than an engine that only explains its engineer, and not only was I stripped of the ambition—just as unrealistic—to transcend literature in my own work (which I like to call "poetic" without that changing anything about its definitively literary nature) but I was also finished with my banal taste for the picturesque and my equally vain desire to play at being an explorer that, while often disguised by less frivolous justifications, had probably been my strongest incentives to travel. At the same time, and without deliberately pursuing a stringent cleansing, I—out of apathy as much as criticism—let go of certain unconditional admirations that were accompanied by a kind of snobbery, such as my Anglomania or my fervor for the bullring, strangers neither to the prestige that Spain enjoyed in the eyes of the *happy few* before it became too touristy nor the dandyism that led me to claim that I was a servant of tragedy's dark beauty. A hidden stain, and the hardest of them to remove: the bad faith that, for various reasons, had gradually tarnished many exaltations that I thought had come from the best part of myself. Creating performances for myself (generally without risk) in which I played the main character, considering myself an exception to every rule (as an excuse): these slant behaviors certainly entered into the ways that, even after I had matured, I had of acting, or not acting, or appearing to act.

If I, due only to attrition, lost my capacity for enthusiasm at the same time that I felt half-robbed of life by the disappearance of my virility and that my silhouette (never so tall in the first place) had begun to shrink, if circumstances independent of myself but that affected me deeply also contributed to narrowing my horizons, couldn't I, on the other hand, congratulate myself for having acquired a more correct perspective and for no longer yielding, for example, to political infatuations (China after Russia, Cuba after China) in which I realized little by little and each time with regret the degree to which we had been duped, myself and others for whom those lures had responded to our need to assign meaning to the world's affairs and to find signs of hope somewhere in that world? Having reached an age where I've shut the door on a pace that continues to accelerate, I can on the whole boast of having progressed on the path toward lucidity and, for that matter, having become less of a conformist, less naïvely subject to the popular ideas of the intellectual milieu to which I began to subscribe as soon as I had crossed the arbitrary threshold of the age of majority—in other words, I can pride myself on being more authentically myself now than I've ever been.

A well-known path, then, whose end I reached as much (if I may say so) through hard work as through the coercion of facts whose lessons I avoided, whatever the cost, until I had been stripped, on a personal level, of numerous mystifications. But can I really congratulate myself for having reached this tabula rasa, if it means finally coming face to face with myself in an absolute void?

◇

The stretch of empty and peaceful plain in the Beauce where, just now, a detail I noticed from far away (the roof of a rather long shed that looked almost white in the cool, late-winter light) made me see—with the very same eye that mutely absorbed the stillness of that building—the silence incapable of making itself heard to affirm that it exists.

◇

When, as a very young child, I learned to read, I soon discovered the very great pleasures and equally great lessons that reading provides: an unknown world opened up to me, and that was more of an initiation than an apprenticeship. But when, at the same time, I took my first steps in writing, I could hardly predict that to write would one day be for me, all questions of entertainment or expertise aside, a means of living in another way, of instantly gaining access to something I will call a *second life*, shamelessly using the expression that Nerval applied to dream to illustrate that it, too, is reality. I use this expression for lack of a better term to describe that uncategorizable state that has for many years been a tonifying experience for me but which I value more and more now that the reality of my life, worn down by time, has grown weaker, and also because, political realities having grown so dark that one can no longer seriously claim to shed any real light upon them, the writer need not be infatuated by "art for art's sake" or consider himself devoted to a calling that exempts him from the world to find himself withdrawing into what his particular activity represents: a wandering stroll taken by thought rather than documentary or ideological content.

That the event becomes writing and that writing, in whatever form it takes, rises to the level of an event, isn't that, after many detours, what I would like to accomplish, driven by sometimes one and sometimes the other of these two desires: to extract, from the real, the imaginary in which I can feel I am living another life, fuller than the real ordinarily is; to infuse the imaginary with enough reality for it to carry at least as much weight as, for many of us, dream carries? A double movement, then: one that essentially obliges me to give poetic color to my experiences; another that urges me, if my construction—pure poetry—falls under the jurisdiction of the récit, to ensure that it possesses enough truth and similarity to anchor itself. Two distinct procedures, but that demonstrate, without the guideline of a narrative, a realist ambition, either that I seek to transfigure (without disfiguring it) a reality or sometimes try to build one from scratch without sinning against verisimilitude or straying from my deep feeling, or that I seek to endow with a kind of real life (which would be as moving as I am moved by it) an impalpability that, originally, existed only nebulously, on a map of words that have yet to be duly adapted or even selected.

I certainly like to read, see, or listen to a work that appears to have transcended artifice and that—because of the singular emotion I feel because of it, touched in the most secret of places and lifted, if I follow the feeling, on a gentle wave modeled upon the universal breath—overwhelms me with the awareness that men—unlike other animals who are incapable of escaping themselves—are able to reach that second life that is not a victory over death but, like an amorous thrill, a way of living more intensely by thinking they're dying a little (or at least ceasing to exist at the mediocre level of the civil state). And yet, I cannot be satisfied unless the work, possibly a modest one, springs directly from myself, a genuine product that expresses who, for too short a time, I am—where I have come from and what order of reality I subscribe to—not the product of someone else's genius that caters to my tastes.

Perhaps this is why I place reading's passivity in opposition to writing, which is necessarily active and keeps me so much more awake that often, at night, when I feel my eyes about to close on the book that grows more and more distant, less real, by the second, whose substance I struggle to absorb, I postpone sleep for an appreciable period of time and set myself, pen in hand, to work.

I must, however, admit that strictly literary writing, a simple preliminary to reading, is in truth only relatively more "active." I also realize that it is quite flimsy to call oneself a realist while only forming bonds with cherry-picked realities (or others that would remain spectral if they weren't concretized into words) and when, no longer able to face the menace of external affairs that grows more haunting almost every day, the writer decides that he will no longer even think about it and stay shut away in his ivory tower from now on, an acceptable way of burying his head in the sand.

◇

How, with my fear of the abyss urging me to try at all costs to bridge the gulf of the irrational, do I elucidate this phrase, conceived one winter morning before I am completely awake:

. . . described (not depicted) in the great barrier symbolizing the ancients.

Described or indicated, as with memory, in skeletal lines. But not *depicted*, painted in a way that would be full enough, fleshy enough, to conjure a presence.

Theatre of operations: the enigmatically named object or figure represented—an allusion scarcely less closed than the cipher, heart or knot of the headless, tailless phrase—by the *ancients*: the deceased crowd of ancestors and elders or juniors who have been KO-ed before us. . . That object or figure with a too-lightly drawn profile: the *barrière grand* (barrier, border, frontier, perhaps a slatted fence or a panel divided into compartments filled with effigies) here inserted in place of the "mère grand," cut philologically from the same cloth and, outside of any grammatical genre, synonymous with the death that is birth's counterpart and from which—now—I am separated only by a transparent barrier.

Perhaps I stand on this questionable threshold when, holding and holding on to my pen as support, I try to make something with the density of a living presence, and not a phantom, rise from the emptiness of the page.

◇

After wondering, when he was very young, how he should write (how to channel words, and which words, to finally produce, poem or prose, something as powerful as a song), he wondered what he should write about (what was worth communicating). Later on, a question that, at first, hadn't troubled him would arise with cruel precision: why write? When the world behaves so badly that moral sanity invites us to risk everything (immediate perils and persecution) to try to change its course, what does it mean to work at giving a mesmerizing tour of the contents of your brain that, divulged with no intention to proselytize but as the pure expression of a sensibility, could only ever slightly change what other people think? And if, by some happy accident, you were to slightly modify that content, what would that change for the world and for you? Furthermore, who, exactly, are these people listening to you? Are they strangers challenged by you, or are they already so like-minded that listening to you amounts to knocking on an open door? Also, if your ambitions run deeper than the charlatan or schoolmaster's, in other words, simply to seduce or instruct, is an authentic need for communion driving you to write and publish your work, or is it instead a sordid desire to make yourself, through it, the object of a louche bond? Paralyzed by these accumulated doubts, he eventually stops writing.

Of course, there's nothing grave about that, since writing is not our only means of dialogue. The concern is that, facing the act of speaking, we will one day find ourselves in an analogous quandary. What forms do we use to articulate, with the right tone and without risking misunderstanding, what is on the tip of our tongue? Did we really know what we were saying, and were we sure that it was worth being said? What interest do we have, anyway, in other peoples' chatter and what good is participating in it by returning the serve? Conversation: most of the time, trifles tossed back and forth like pieces of change or bartered merchandise. When faced with another person, we must say something, if only to demonstrate that we are able to speak and that we are superior to animals, plants, and stones because of it. But why, when all is said and done, must we prove that we are human beings? Doesn't proving it give it a meaning that it doesn't really have? Also, wishing to sound intelligent, we end up keeping quiet, except for the necessities surrounding eating, drinking and sleeping. Inertia that soon reaches this limit: without the support of words to pronounce, we no longer string words together, even internally.

While we have at least followed this kind of trajectory in theory, isn't returning to the starting point and trying, in practice, to resolve the question of *how* to write an attempt to seek shelter from the vertiginous cascade that, from *how* into *why*, makes us tumble into the abyss or weave our way through the most venomous of question marks? But it would be absurd to hope to get away with that scheme, for we cannot raise the question of *how* without, at the same time, awakening all the others.

In its dappled singularity, *l'Asperge* painted by the observing, transfiguring Édouard Manet seemed just as refined as—motif of a different painting—the flower he placed in a tall, narrow crystal vase (like the glass holding two roses in front of the beautiful blonde barmaid at the *Bar aux Folies-Bergère*), as translucent as the champagne flutes found not only in many private homes but at Tortoni, the famous café that the artist frequented for many years.

In a similar way, pebbles, shoemaker's leather, and army trousers democratically participate in Stephane Mallarmé's panoply that showcases, alongside living and immediately sensual elements, the mirror, the fan, and dice.

They say of Olympia's author, also revolutionary in his art and capable of extracting a jewel from the most modest motif, that he was a witty and elegant man, but that his relatively easy life—apart from his illness—made him a character who was certainly distinguished but also a bit self-effacing. Couldn't we say almost the same thing about his friend, the poet Stéphane Mallarmé, the respectable high-school teacher with bad reviews, who only set off firecrackers on the blank page—as others do on rooftops—and, it seems, only read his poems aloud in all their glory on those famous Tuesdays at rue de Rome or in front of a few friends?

◇

In my right hand,
my obsession to manipulate,
dismantle,
displace and amalgamate words,
mammaries immemorial
that I suck on, gasping for breath.

Barbarous murmurs, in my Babel
you keep me drunk in your care
and, a chattering boor, I babble.

In the left hand,
my contraptions,
my thingamajigs,
my wedges,
the worries (froufrous and chinoiseries) that pick fights with me,
my antics, mummeries, and moralisms.

In the middle,
the slack ache that grinds me,
bites me,
screws me,
undoes me,

humiliates me
and that, bitter honey, I make into a mishmash to simmer, marinate,
macerate.

Did he say that this demented world demands denial,
that demon who shrouds, entangles and dismantles me?

◇

There are conversations in which it would seem, given their substance, that everything had been said, that nothing had been omitted from what, at the time, should and could have been said. And yet, it often happens that such a conversation leaves you wanting more; eager to communicate, you spoke with all the sincerity and all the intelligence you were capable of, your interlocutor demonstrating, in return, as much intelligence and sincerity as was shown by your own remarks; and yet nothing happened, you and presumably the other remained neutral, even if you reached an agreement. What kept the spark from igniting and uniting the two poles? Perhaps it was the tone, the accent, the modulation, together with a small gesture or the quasi-imperceptible play of physiognomy, in short an imponderable that outweighed the conversation, perhaps that's what, in even the most mundane conversations, enables complicity. . . Communicating is not a trade (a matter of exchange or give-and-take) but finding yourselves in tune and sharing—albeit in the absence of any serious debate or any confidence worthy of mention—an intimate resonance.

◇

Odorize,
glow,
glimmer,
gleam,
shimmer,
flavor,
vibrate,
resonate,
pulsate,
radiate,

what verb (an invention) could summarize all of these words to—grasping and emboldening it—designate the quality that would make these pages as voluble as Olympia, adorned by her thin black ribbon?

$\diamond$

The most famous work of that great latecomer to (or, according to his devotees, modern pioneer of) genre painting was named *The Dogon in a Gondola*. In a Venetian setting—characterized by the Rialto bridge whose two peaks, crowned by two cheerful arcades, brighten the painting's background—we see a Black African, apparently very tall, fairly thin, and with a graying beard, in a gondola. At his feet is a small travel bag, similar to those his congeners use to transport the cheap paintings they spread out on the city's sidewalks to offer them for sale. In his arms is an object whose ethereal delicacy and height (only several meters tall, but suggesting the reach of the pyramids) rivals the grandest of palaces: a mask of the "multi-story" variety, the most spectacular of those used by the Dogons in their funeral dances.

The painter's enormous talent was apparent in the way he knew how to structure the work by playing the obtuse, broken line between the bridge and the man's back against the vertical line created by the long openwork plank of the mask. A skilled colorist, he had chosen a palette that was seductive despite its austerity, comprised of the same colors traditionally used to decorate the "multi-story" masks: black, white and red. These three colors were visible in every part of the painting, as the artist had set the scene under a leaden (dull gray) sky and a

181

beautiful setting sun, a few rays of which, piercing the cloud cover, cast reddened reflections on the somber waters of the Grand Canal between the buildings, soberly treated in black and white as if it were enough to remind us that they were there, inert witnesses of a bustling human swarm whose muddle of variegated colors we could only imagine. Neither yellow nor blue were included in the color scheme and its only dissonance—minimal but striking—was introduced by the burnt sienna tunic in which (to the great pleasure of the eye) the Dogon peddler was dressed, crowned by a sort of Phrygian bonnet magisterially indicated by a few liberal brushstrokes in nearly the same shade of brown.

If this painting, monumental in scale despite its small size, had been actually realized and considered by its author to be complete, it should have—in my view—been signed in red or pure white on the side of the black gondola. But since it is even less real than a memory, it was not signed, unless perhaps by me, its inventor, who might have (like those artists of our era who use this method to announce that the work is above all a document) followed my first and last name with the abbreviated date of its creation: *11–3–77*. But, if I explicitly claim responsibility for this fictional canvas, shouldn't I also mention that it implicitly constitutes an "Homage to Raymond Roussel," since it was starting from a play on words—which reared its head while I was sitting at the barber's during one of our brief Friday morning appointments—and using a process identical to the one whose secret Roussel revealed in a work that became a posthumous book, that *The Dogon in a Gondola* was composed? Returning to the date and its concise notation (which showed me something I otherwise never would have seen), I find that the 77 of a century ago was the birth year of that writer who has been ignored for far too long, and I discover (an even more unusual thing) that 11 multiplied by 3 makes 33, which leads to

1933, the date of his probably intentional death in Palermo, an Italian port resembling the precarious Venice, one of whose most picturesque locations appeared in the painting. Thus, the gondolier whose presence I only suggested in order to indicate the Dogon and situate the gondola—that indispensable boatman whom I left in shadow, as if a taboo prohibited me from showing him except in silhouette—took on the sinister form of Charon, which would be, without my having intended it, the full significance of the mask as an instrument associated with funereal rites, and whose verticality was underscored by the elegant line of the bridge.

And so, it is without thinking of anything other than giving substance to something that had previously existed only as an outline of verbal music that, on the year of his uncelebrated centenary, I will have paid homage to someone who—another coincidence—died on July 14th, the 11 + 3rd day of the seventh month (the 7 of the 77 that, when its two numerals are added together, equals the same fateful 14), while the initial 11 reduced to a single 1 suggests the first month of the year, the January in which he was born; and moreover, I also notice that a need to identify my main character as a Dogon by providing a hairstyle and an obviously illustrative object steered me towards the quasi-Phyrigian hat and the three colors (which could easily be those of a flag) that are evocative of everything that our July 14th holiday claims to commemorate. Objective chance, I might call it—were I less aware of my interpretive bias—using the vocabulary of that other vanished soul, André Breton, who may not have studied the initiatory language rites of the Dogons as I have but was one of the first to recognize the genius of the author of *Impressions of Africa*.

And yet, my debt to Raymond Roussel is not the only one I have to settle. *The Dogon in a Gondola* could have been the seed of a very different iconographically descriptive text, if the memory of another imaginary painting (one pertaining to the Paris Commune) hadn't awoken somewhere inside me, *la Belle Versaillaise* as it emerged fully formed from the mind of Pierre Klossowski, not only a writer but an illustrator and "genre" painter who, if he had chosen to, in the curiously erotic style from which I believe he never strayed, could have given color and form to his Versaillaise: a pearl in the oyster of the arcades reflecting the Tuileries fire in the distance, an intoxicating young woman molested in the rue de Rivoli by two representatives of the angry mob. But I can only write my Dogon with an unmagical hand—if I wish to endow him with some semblance of reality by granting him the status of a visible image—and I ought to keep myself from portraying him through anything other than allusions and ambiguous touches. Wouldn't messing around with his portrait too much, trying to embellish it with charming details, hit a wrong note that an expert who hails from the region in question would have every right to sneer at?

Finally, wishing that none of the underlying facts of this Venetian scene go unmentioned, I add that the salt-and-pepper goatee of the traveler who looked as if he were all muscle and nerve and the chestnut brown tunic that stood out against the blackness of the skiff were also worn by Ambara Dolo, my old Dogon contact, whom I saw again after more than thirty years when he was brought to Paris by an ethnologist he had worked with for many years and who wanted to help cure him of a terrible illness he had in his chest. When we saw each other again, Ambara Dolo—who, despite the care he received, passed away shortly afterwards in the village full of flat-roofed houses in which he was a local dignitary—shared with me that, when his two wives had asked him if it was a good idea for him travel to Paris at his age, he had nonchalantly replied, "Death is everywhere."

"The magician has come back. . . He's going on his treasure hunt. . ." the school's headmistress announced, as she entered the dining room of the boarding house where I had arrived the afternoon the day before; the school had given out awards that morning, a fact that was discreetly announced by the building's decorations and the formal dress worn by many people in the street. I had come for a three-day visit to Terre-de-Haut, one of the islands near Guadeloupe that were Christianly baptized "The Saints" and inhabited by people who, in this area, surprise almost everyone with their remarkably pale skin. Not Saintoise but Guadeloupian, the woman who had just announced the good news and who at the midday meal had also mentioned a sorcerer (this same magician, perhaps) was a fat, tan woman whose breasts were too heavy and figure was too thick, but she had a rather beautiful, slightly Oriental face, framed by two large gold rings that hung from her ears. She was accompanied by her nurse—an elderly woman of color, somewhat shriveled but cheerful and distinguished—and a very young black girl, a sweet little airhead dressed as the two others were in a pretty, light dress that was suitable to that climate. As for the magician whose arrival was announced by the opulent Guadeloupian as if he were a celebrity, he showed up just as dinner began: a main-lander of some 45 or 50 years, going gray, looking dapper and pontificating about two islands in the north of Guadeloupe where I have spent some time: Saint-Barthélemy (which he said was very similar to Saintes, which would have been correct if he hadn't neglected to mention that the northern island, populated by Normans who have remained almost completely unassimilated, is far superior to the southern one, which is just as complex and picturesque but whose landscapes are less expansive, and don't give the same impression of being bizarrely faraway), Saint-Martin (the half-Dutch, half-French island where, as our dinner companion observed, as many others have, public services are far better organized on the Dutch side than on the French). Over the course of the conversation, I learned that this phoenix of the dinner table, this magician whose return the amiable headmistress who had lived there for four years and was preparing to leave for a "change of scene" appeared to celebrate as a seasonal event, was only a vacationing illusionist. Later, I would learn that he was a native of Burgundy, an origin that his accent should have been enough for me to identify.

I find these details, which my memory wasn't able to provide, in the seventh notebook of the travel journal I kept during the entirety of this trip (a mission that Unesco had charged me with in 1952 to study the state of relations between the different racial categories of the French Antilles population). These notes, the majority of which were taken at night and whose recapitulation brought my day to a close, recounted not only the interviews I had taken with people of every color and social status that the investigation required, but all of my comings and goings, even if they were purely for pleasure. Thus, in Terre-de-Haut, I neglected neither the walks that, crossing meadows and passing a few cows here and there, took me to the edges of the coastline, nor—in the center of town—my stops at the Coq d'or, a café with a billiards table and a terrace where, when I was tired of running around, I could drink a beer in peace (brought to me by Berthe, a chloritic waitress who was ornery and slightly brutish, like someone working in a sailor bar on the Manche or the North Sea except that, a daughter of the tropics, she liked to work barefoot when business was slow) and, while refreshing myself on the balcony that overlooked the pier, enjoy the spectacle of the street, which was always enticing and sometimes instructive. I was also not averse to noting down exotic touches, details of flora or fauna I had noticed during these outings of mine (for example, varieties of green pumpkins that bristled with thorns and were crowned by a purplish-blue and red bulb that also was covered with thorns, cactuses called "Turk's Heads"/"Têtes d'Anglais" which I couldn't distinguish from the ones called "Bishop's Hats" in Saint-Martin, and even, on the beach, the sand crabs that, mostly yellow but some of an opalescent blue, would emerge from their holes, prick up their two little black eyes, and go back where they came from walking sideways, sometimes very quickly, rising up on their pincers like dancers on pointe).

All of this—and I am mortified by it—hardly exists except in writing. I go back, for example, to what I said about Berthe the servant, I recopy it almost word for word, keeping to the romanticism that inspired me to poeticize the model, but that isn't what allows me to see her again as she was. The figure of another servant—whom I met over the course of the same trip but I no longer know where, maybe in Martinique, someone whose complexion was indisputably tropical—overtakes and nearly eclipses her completely, even though this other woman was so unoriginal that I'm not even sure if her silhouette appears in any of my notebooks. While the magician, with his wand, was more distinctive, he did not escape this disintegration and I remember almost nothing about him except for what I find in these notes. Only the image of a clean-shaven face and a torso clad in a white shirt with short or rolled-up sleeves comes back to me, and I wouldn't be able to swear to its perfect accuracy.

One paragraph of the notebook that recounts my trip to Les Saintes (a fragment of a memory-aid in which things drawn from life or something to that effect are planted as if in a herbarium and to which I can refer, but without those notes written in cursive springing to life as I reread them or emerging from their documentary coldness to help me as much as I would like them to when I try to positively remember them) describes the magician bringing back a lizard, easily two feet long, that he had mortally wounded with a shot from a small six-millimeter pistol, then summarizes the interview that I had done with a Tartarin and a young White Guadeloupian, probably indigent, who worked in Basse-Terre. As the headmistress of the school had said, the magician—perhaps inspired by tales of the buccaneers and the Antilles' turbulent past—hunted for treasure by using, he told us, an American device that detected metals but didn't give any quantitative indication of them, and so it was easy to exhume, instead of treasure, a bolt or an old can of sardines. Regarding his profession—which I asked him about, curious as to what a professional has to say—the illusionist insisted that it was essentially a matter of "psychology" and then cited several authorities who, according to him, were members of the society of prestidigitators: the president Édouard Herriot, the professor Locart (from Lyon), and a bishop who, as a missionary, had used his talents to garner great respect from the residents of Gabon, but had to provide an explanation of the matter to the Holy See.

The next day, July 14—a date that I read in my notebook, followed by no allusion to any specific festivities—I began my day with a swim in the ocean, taken as soon as I woke up in Marigot Bay on an absolutely deserted beach surrounded entirely by manchineels, those trees that legend claims are dangerous because of the corrosive sap they exude. Before reaching a large,

probably saltwater pond, a vast and almost perfectly round surface that was yellowish in color and studded with tufts of grass,
I passed a much smaller pond on my right, this one fenced off
and equipped God knows why with a turnstile (perhaps a way,
I realize while rereading, to keep cattle away from this little
pool). The mantle of plants and aquatic flowers that covered it
looked so opaque that I thought of the death of Ophelia,
steeped as I was in the memory I had of the island of St.
Barthelemy, which was at one time Scandinavian and whose
principal agglomeration is still named Gustavia, a Hamletizing
memory that I would quite naturally project onto the Saints,
Pont-Aven of the Tropics, or Paimpol Tahiti (as my report, literary
for once, calls them). Second walk and second swim, this time
in a bay that must have, I presume, been part of the Pont-Pierre
bay—a name that to me is nothing more than a name—where I
dove into the water to escape the reach of pollen that would
have completely permeated my clothes, which I thought it better to strip myself of and hide (sheltering them in the bottom of
a boat). Took a walk in the opposite direction—towards the
Coquelet cove—and a quick survey of a purely artisanal construction site where boats were built, then on the way back, near
the unmarked police station, I met a retired minor dignitary I
had seen the night before at the home of the parish priest;
wearing a large hat in the Indochine style (a sort of a thick waf-
fle of basketwork wrapped in white fabric, the kind that some
men and women wear here) this old, fat mulatto, who just the
other day was whining about how immoral the Saintois had
become, was lamenting the absence of flags, lecturing to a group
of fishermen who obviously didn't give a damn about it. Third
outing a little later, accompanied by the illusionist, Mr.
Boulogne, the young white man from yesterday, and someone
named de Beaupré, a bearded and spectacled importer who didn't
hide the fact that he preferred the merchants of the old Basse-Terre

to the Pointe-à-Pitre, since their prices were less exorbitant. With nothing to do, and not wanting to appear to be snubbing my comrades, I agreed to go up with them to Fort Napoléon, which I had visited the morning of the day before, armed with a key that I had to request from the police station, and where I had to cross a drawbridge before walking down a large arched corridor that led to the entrance, which was barred by a heavy door. The rampart walk was haunted, along with numerous lizards and many rarer iguanas, by fat birds that sometimes took off with a sudden, startling flapping of wings—and presented an overview broad enough for a rambling eye to land upon many variously beautiful sights (coves, islands, promontories, etc., plus a meadow that made you want to graze in it and a large pool of water barely separated from the sea).

At the end of the day—at six o'clock, according to these notes that now evoke so little that they almost seem like an inventory of things that someone else experienced or collected—was the dance-hall performance of Freddy Reys, the illusionist, which I had assured him I would attend. He had once again bragged at lunch about his knowledge of the Antilles, assuring me—he knew from experience—that the residents of Martinique were more stubborn than the Guadeloupeans. As I usually do with unsolicited remarks, I noted this not as information in which I should place any credence but as one opinion among others that were likely to illuminate me on the state of mind, persuasion, economic standing, or origin of the person who articulated it.

As for the performance that started an hour late (the proverbial Antilles lateness, even though the promoter was a mainlander), I wrote down nothing about it that allows me, after 25 years, to have any idea of what, technically, it contained. In truth, I don't think the program included any breathtaking marvels and that the tricks of its peculiar star were little more than deft and clever hand manipulations. My dinner companion of the past several days would probably have required greater financial means than those available to him to present tricks that demanded a high production value.

While he failed to impress us with his astounding talent, as we had every right to expect, Freddy Reys showed an undeniable work ethic. A true jack-of-all-trades performing a one-man show*, he did it all: greeted the public, seated the audience that barely fit into the small, shabby room, and quieted the crowd; before taking the stage, he simultaneously played cashier, usher, and security guard. At one point during his act, which unfolded before a decidedly restless audience, this shrewd psychologist thought it was a good idea, in an attempt to quiet things down, to tell the audience off in no uncertain terms, not hesitating to call them "savages" and declaring, at the height of his brief diatribe, that he thought he was in Guadeloupe, in France, and not in a country full of savages. At the time, the audience didn't seem to react, but after the performance, as the audience dispersed I heard many protest, naturally, against the insults that this buffoon had directed at them.

A diluvian rain, which began falling during the performance, continued during our exit and several of us took refuge in a tiny shed where we found two goats bleating incessantly, frightened by the storm. That's when I overheard (this I remember as vividly as the trivial incident that will eventually humiliate my travel companion once and for all) the vehement arguing of two or three men of color whom I assumed to be fishermen because of their clothes. It wasn't really an argument, though; while it was virulent in tone, the men agreed that the magician had made a mockery of everyone in the audience and his magic was nothing but deception. "It's all just tricks!" if my memory is correct, was what one participant in this obvious "babbling" (a tremendous argument, in crude language, using violent words and gesticulations) said. Ignoring the entire art of illusionism—the creation of illusions with which the spectator is happy to play along—these philistines, who had come to see a magician, were outraged by having seen only an amiable crook whose work was based on subtle maneuvers that were designed to deceive. More stubborn than the Gabonese, who were supposedly appeased by prestidigitation they believed was real magic, they rebelled, headstrong, against alleged magic that turned out to be prestidigitation, and thus was nothing but a sham.

As for myself, who only saw the under-appreciated show-man two days later, since he hadn't shown up for dinner at the boarding house where his place at the table, as it was at lunch, had been set, I realized that my way of thinking hadn't been all that different from the two or three dissenters who were disappointed by the show's protagonist—and they were obviously not alone—because they had expected much more from him than they could logically expect from a member of his profession. Returning to Basse-Terre the way I had arrived, aboard *la Belle Saintoise*, a modest sailboat with a motor that on Tuesdays and Wednesdays stopped at Terre-de-Haut and its twin sister Terre-de-Bas to transport passengers, mail, and cargo, I saw—right in the middle of the Saintes Canal, an inlet where pitching and rolling were the norm—poor Freddy Reys, on the same boat crammed with cases of empty bottles of beer and lemonade, some of which had been brought by the pale Berthe as the boat was boarding, suddenly squat down and projectile vomit, with enough correctness (and I must give him credit for this) not to spray any of his fellow passengers. Not too far away, two men of color observed the scene and burst out laughing. As for myself, this incident surprised me beyond reason: while I certainly did not demand that an illusionist be a magician, I believed that this man's disconcerting savoir-faire made him extraordinary enough—like a hero made invulnerable by an anointing of dragon's blood—that he would be immune to seasickness. While in this case, the concerned party hadn't even been able to spirit away, by a sleight-of-hand trick, the humiliating results. . .

MEA CULPA:

A note by Raymond Queneau, discovered and published in a bulletin devoted to his memory, relates how he overheard the audience in a Parisian music hall rant and rave, with cries of "Fraud! Fraud!," against an illusionist who was sawing a woman locked in a coffin in half.

This testimony—which I was not aware of until long after I had written my own testimony concerning the Saintoise fisher-men—shows me that they had no monopoly on the type of blindness that Queneau described. Was I prompted by a bit of unconscious racism when I spoke of them as if, in the Antilles, certain people were likely to demonstrate more naiveté than a métropolitan audience?

The final obstacle to total nudity, excluding the jewel on her wrist and the mules about to fall off her feet: the neck-ribbon—almost a thread—whose knot, as elegant as the seal on a package containing a gift, forms a double loop above the sumptuous offering of her two breasts that looks as if it could be undone merely by pulling on one of its ends.

More than just an ornament, this bauble that, for Manet, was perhaps nothing more than a capricious black line cutting through the whiteness of the nude, is for us the unnecessary detail that hooks us and makes *Olympia* real.

Just like the object that, a foreign body joined to a living body whose presence it reinforces, gives the fetishist a hard-on.

While looking, just the other day on the rue de Flandre, at those two enormous buildings each of which at a certain height begin to flare out (a water tower in the shape of a funnel, a castle with excessively hypertrophied machicolations, the festooned stern of a sailboat from the days of the buccaneers, a musket turned towards the sky, Jericho's trumpet raised to make it crumble), I felt euphoria swelling within me: a movement of ascension and broadening—my heart a hot-air balloon, my lungs wings unfolding—quite different from the sensation unleashed by tall barracks with vertical walls whose view, instead of liberating you, gives you the feeling of being held prisoner in a cluster of mercilessly stiff, parallel lines.

Even though the rue de Flandres is relatively far from my home, I could easily go back and visit those two buildings I had only seen in passing and whose majesty, for only a moment, I had admired. I could certainly improve upon my impulsive description. . .

But I'd bet that I wouldn't recapture my first impression if I did, and I might even ask myself how the sight had ever enthralled me to such a degree! Uninterested in playing the role of a modern architecture critic—or even in giving my approval, for once—I will not return to that street where, while it may be busy, nothing evokes the opulence that the cloth industry once bestowed upon many cities in Flanders.

◇

What, in fact, am I pursuing?

—The combination of words, phrases, sequences, etc. that only I can cobble together and that—in my life, like every other, on an island whose living conditions are in a constant state of decline—would be my vade-mecum for the castaway, my version of everything that allowed Robinson to survive: pencil case, Bible, even Friday (if I should end up living a solitary life and lack the heart to apply the categorical remedy).

. . . Or rather, what fascinates me is less the result, and the help that I theoretically expect from it, than the bricolage itself, whose supposed goal is, when all is said and done, only a pretext. At the exact point where things are inside as much as outside of me, what other than this *hobby** could keep me from becoming a Robinson who, once his work is done, simply nods off into sleep, without even looking at the sea?

◇

Through travel (living somewhere other than the place we are accustomed to, as a cow is to its pasture),

through noctambulism (which, by replacing day with night, overturns time and creates a sort of inverted world),through alcohol or any other substance (whose consumption intoxicates us and takes us out of ourselves),

through a performance so captivating that we project ourselves into it completely,

through any practice, adventure, or magic spell that disrupts routine, it's good to get disoriented. Once you break the chain, life unfolds as if, through a bath of unfamiliar sensations and ideas, your mind, laid bare, rediscovers the powers it had been gradually deprived of by quotidian rust.

Naturally, none of this opposes the way using only what we have at hand, we discover exotic substances within ourselves and how, without leaving our current surroundings or even lifting a finger, we may explore lands so distant and uncertain that they're guaranteed to be rich in surprises. And yet we must understand that it is certainly easier to let circumstances shake us up and cause, at least for a short time, our imagination to soar than to incite this internal revolution—lasting barely longer than a lightning flash—without the aid of something to divert us from the ordinary, clear away our lethargy, and give us a running start.

◇

Splitting the double row of massive edifices, tiers of organ pipes that vary in size, form, and material, wide, straight avenues bathed in the tender light of a slightly humid summer sink into the distance until they disappear from view, cut crosswise by minor arteries and so long, you might say, that following them to their extraordinarily distant vanishing point would take a lifetime. New York thoroughfares in an ambiguous model of the future, for the eye's prow.

At the Philadelphia museum, eyes glued to the pair of holes drilled into the rustic door that masks Marcel Duchamp's assemblage, *Étant donnés: 1° la chute d'eau, 2° le gaz d'eclairage*, I saw—a desire that had been nagging at me for a while—the naked female mannequin who, carrying a lamp resembling the Auer lamps of yesteryear, appears voluptuously splayed out in a vernal landscape whose photographic quality and absolute banality of color accentuates the discomfort that the viewer already feels because of its bawdy means of discovery.

Here, it isn't a black ribbon tied around the neck but an unusual detail, the actual light held in her right hand, that confers a disarming presence upon this life-size mannequin whose head and feet are invisible, obscured from view by the intact portion of the crumbling wall through which the spectacle presents itself. The figure, then, doubly truncated, as fragmented as a lifeless torso on a battlefield, is thus confirmed as an object of pure physical adoration.

To my great displeasure, even though I studied it closely, I failed to notice the waterfall that, apparently, sparkles—rather distantly—in a corner of the principally vegetal scene.

After more than an entire day of storms—the sky in demolition, torrential downpours, the incessant growling of obstinate thunder—overcast hours followed by even longer periods of stormy weather with only brief reprieves, the sun, with one stroke of the brush, rekindled the colors of the majestic palaces and dilapidated houses of Rome, dead bodies pierced here and there by the ivory skeletons of ruins. But that couldn't brighten my mood, for it had deteriorated almost to the point of collapse by my return to that city that had become so dangerous at night and (according to many warnings) questionable even in the middle of the day, that memorable city that, in those first two weeks of October 1980, spoke literally nothing to me except noise, disorder, the indiscretion of the botched work on its monuments and the triviality of its tourist cattle calls, even though its luminosity had once given such eloquent responses to my anxious cries.

Still, it's ungracious to begrudge a city for not being what it once was, and to ignore its beautiful remainders, when it is just one of the many mirrors that reflect how you, too, are decaying!

◇

Which aromatics with unique powers and intoxicating scents could preserve what I wrap up in these lines that are less ribbons than strips, embalming a pharaoh with no other kingdom than the papyrus that lacks any and all relief?

To write by hand instead of on the typewriter so that it is this hand—one of the parts of our body that we feel belongs to us most directly—that with no intermediary other than the fountain pen (less intrusive than a keyboard, because it is a simple appendage to the fingers), crafts the lines letter by letter and clings to them, as if each of them and even each of the written signs should be, on the one hand, a direct affirmation of life (as much as graffiti or another mark indicating that we had, one day, been there) and, on the other, a pole we grab hold of, in full muscular awareness of the gesture, to keep from drowning.

Despite the effort to *write well* (to speak in the most penetrating and convincing way possible, casting a magic spell), this still-fresh writing appears to concern a waking dream more than it does literature. And yet, a mutation occurs when—after the stage of the typewritten copy, already anonymous and dislocated even though it will be corrected by hand just as the proofs, at another stage, will be—the manuscript, passing from the private to the public domain, will have become a printed text, ensconced in the organization of its characters and dressed as it must to be sent to whomever it may concern and sold in bookstores. And so this series of pages, vital to us and hence priceless, turns out in the end to be a banal, commercial product: larger but geometrically of the same family as the sugar cube and matchbox, a dry paperback with cut pages, the last avatar of what only yesterday we pictured as surrounded by rays of light like the Tablets of Stone.

While we're in the thick of it, we would like the book, a tossed pebble, to make some waves. But, whatever acclaim it may receive, the party will already be over, the spell already broken. And so, at the risk of foundering, we can only try, picking up up pen and paper, to begin again.

Don't we also close ourselves up in that circle when, falling in love with the art of writing and fascinated by the manipulation of words, we forget that before it was a recourse for us, writing had once been a way to clarify and share with others?

◇

Ribbon at Olympia's throat, the black-on-white lines I write should, at every moment, evoke a presence. And yet, my problem isn't so much that: less circumscribed, my challenge—which is only of expression—is instead to catch, as with a lasso that grips them at just the right spot, the things that are present enough for me to be able, by transmission, to make their presence known.

Acting first and foremost on the stage of capture and not of harness, the lasso—obviously—has the upper hand on the ribbon.

And isn't it always something *savage* (crude, naked, untouched, even unruly) that this lasso should capture, both outside and inside myself?

◇

When—believing that the word holds the answer to the question—I speak of "presence" regarding a work of art, am I keeping, if not to explication, at least to the main idea? Or am I simply noting that this thing, the fruit of an imagination working with materials originally prepared by common experience (forms, colors, volumes in the visual arts, sounds and rhythms in music, language in literature), that this work, created by mortals at every level but whose effect is nevertheless a mystery, achieves a reality that not only exceeds the reality of the materials that are transmuted by it but that feels more powerful to me than the majority of the realities that surround it? Escaping the ghetto of the imaginary, it makes us feel—intensely—that it exists, and sets itself apart entirely in real life, rather than simply playing a hand in a game that—although brilliant—remains closed in on itself.

One can imagine one's life in the form of a novel or a symphony; harder to think of it as a game of chess or a rugby match. And even if you can equate whatever action you may be performing with a poker play, that will only be an image: while theoretically interesting, the ideal poker play you refer to will only be an abstract element of comparison and, since it can only participate as such, won't share the carnal resonance of a work that seems to reveal a bit of yourself, and that moves you enough that its memory, repeatedly returning to you with living heat and breath, becomes your escort. In other words, as opposed to gambling and sports, art is a language that says more and goes further than what, objectively, is said. A language whose most striking examples show, in the present moment, undeniable realities that, over time, continue to haunt you and in so doing retain a kind of presence after the initial shock has passed. Language that is all the more *active* because you find it to be more *actual*, close to your state at the moment and in manifest agreement with the world in which you live at that moment— language thus gifted with a modernity that is not simply a matter of fashion and that derives neither from a naive cult of Progress nor an avant-garde itch, but is the result of works that, rising above everything that separates us from the very heart of our existence as it is objectively lived, arrive at just the right moment to somehow back us into a corner of our reality, which can only exist in the present. Works that, singularly moving and educational, can—and museums are living proof of this—date from another era but to a large degree are no less "modern" in the sense that they seem to relate directly to our present reality, and that this other era, purely historical or at least dormant in our memory, seems as real, as present to us as if we were united with it in a relationship without retrospection.

Perhaps the first condition for an artist of yesterday or today is to assert himself as being fiercely present in his own time, to bewitch us by steeping us in the notion that as different as he may be from us, he is moving at exactly the same pace as we are (or should be) moving and, placing all personal considerations aside, exacts that acute feeling of relevance that so many of our contemporaries are unable to give us. For whoever undertakes one of these activities that are less akin to play than to magic— since they tend to hypnotize the people who watch, read, or listen to their work—it would be relatively easy, then, to know essentially which path to take, if there weren't so many different, and often less obvious, ways to assert oneself as being *present in one's time* and if, also, it weren't nearly impossible to evaluate this era in which tidal waves from various directions continue to collide. And then, to add insult to injury, there is always the risk that these activities, even the most uncompromising and revolutionary of them, are now only amiable relics of a bygone era compared to the phraseless revolt that our current era demands.

◇

Am I
    a leafless tree
    an oxidized wine
    a dethroned king
    a naked animal
    a spumeless wave
    a marble no longer streaked by exhausted dreams?

$\diamond$

Anxious (it seems) about what her boss will say or do and coddling her with a glance that might lead us to think that Olympia, whose gaze towards her audience seems indifferent to everything it sees, was only created to be gazed upon, is this gloomy maid the only person whom the painting, hiding nothing and yet charged with mystery, depicts as motivated by a definable emotion?

In her orbit, in fact, we find nothing but an icy beauty that, as indifferent to the bouquet offered to her as Salomé was to the head of the anchorite, seems to be there exclusively to be there, in her absolute presence, and an animal—a cat—whose thoughts, more concealed than they are expressed by his frozen stare, elude us to the point that we can hardly imagine what obscure plan he has in mind, even the least articulable.

◇

The moment that reconciles you without anything seeming to have appointed it: we recognize its nature not in the present but the past, in the retrospective glance that places us—lucid—in its presence.

Needed: to abolish this interval and realize a simultaneity of thunder and lightning that falls at your feet.

Writing in the present (or that claims to be in the present), poetry—without telling a story—invokes the presence of something that was once present for you or—even less of a story—speaks of no event other than its own advent. And yet, language is based on a past tense: words that previously existed and that, shaped by their extended adventures, carry along with them a mass of sedimentary meanings and, conjugated with other words in a play of assonance, gradually dredge up a wide range of old sensations and feelings within us. It is devoted to anachronism from the very start.

Could it be from this contradiction, assumed but not resolved, between the novelty of construction and the obsolescence of materials—between the unexpected punishment that the inventor forces them to endure and the nostalgic traces with which they are charged—that a poetic text draws its power?

◇

Between hide and flesh,
between dog and wolf,
between two waters,
between two flames.

◇

In that distant era when—guided by someone who has in some way shaped my life, since without his example and support I would not have worked in the museum of ethnology where I still work today even though the mood there has grown somewhat oppressive, someone who was able, thanks to the diversity of his gifts, to take his slender silhouette of an anchorite or a funambulist pretty much everywhere, to circulate in the most serious as well as the most frivolous company, and who, enmeshed in the obscure group of artists and writers to which I then belonged, had become its Barnum, as it were—I made some feeble appearances in what is called the "world" (a curious appellation, for it seems to imply that the universe is reduced to the social circle it designates, a narrow and poorly defined milieu with no precise criteria in place for its borders), I was always surprised by the way in which the banal expression, "Comment allez-vous?" ["How are you?"] was pronounced by the men and women who appeared to set the tone.

Abstaining from pronouncing the link that proper usage demands between the final syllable of the adverb (that orthography equips with a final *t*) and the first of the verb (in this case the vowel *a*), they omitted the t and, following the first word with an infinitesimal pause, articulated the second as if it had opened on a lightly aspirated *h*—in short, they used an expression that would have been transcribed empirically not as "Comment" followed by "tallez-vous" without a break, but "Commen(t) hallez-vous." Certainly, politeness may have had something to do with it (elaborating the phrase so it wouldn't seem too mechanical). But what better way to affirm that you belong to a privileged class than to adopt, at least in certain cases, an accent so uncommon that it could pass as foreign without anyone being able to identify its original country or territory!

Since then—and I say this without regret or the slightest bit of pride, as I have hardly any biases in this regard and even believe that snobbism, in the domain of the arts, although too sheeplike and superficial to practice indiscriminately, can help to disseminate new ideas, not without some efficacy although sometimes at a degrading price—I have lived at too great a distance from worldliness to know if this way of eliminating the link that the philistine expects to hear was only a fashion, even the prerogative of a clique, or if the custom has endured. I've uttered and heard many "Comment allez-vous" without thinking for even a second about the way in which my interlocutor or I pronounced them, and without attaching any importance to the question, which is so conventional that it's slightly surprising and almost bad form to respond with anything other than, "Very well, thanks, and you?" unless, even more lazily, you merely repeat the question.

And yet, one or two years ago if not more, I noticed that when, in the public institution where they have been kind enough to let me keep my office even though I reached the age of retirement some time ago, a colleague or another member of the staff asked me how I was, he used a very specific tone of voice. He didn't affect an accent that characterized it as unusual or engage in a posh kind of slang, but it seemed—at least this was the impression that I got, although I may have imagined it—that he was asking me an actual question instead of stating, quasi-mechanically, that "How are you?" that is even less of a conversational element than a hello or a goodbye. I certainly appreciated the intonation's kindness, but I was a bit annoyed by it as well and, dare I say it, both offended and vaguely disconcerted by it: despite what I see (an illusion, of course) in the mirror, am I now so decrepit that it would be normal that I not feel well, and that there would then be some occasion, for someone who actually isn't the least bit interested in me, to approach me and ask me directly, and not while absentmindedly applying a protocol, about the state of my health? Until now, I could always respond—with a few exceptions—in a reassuring enough way for the conversation not to continue upon that theme. But how long will that last? Will there come a day when someone will say, "Au revoir" with a nuance of worried doubt, as if seeing me again was an eventuality that my advanced age rendered problematic?

◇

Shorter and skinnier than the heavy barges that are often stationed on this Parisian arm of the Seine, a scow with a British flag on its stern, unstylish but surely recreational, if not by vocation at least in its current state—was docked for several days below our apartment windows, which are outfitted with screens to protect against the traffic noise that, frankly, is outrageous here. Three young men occupied it, whom we watched as they strolled around in dark blue sweaters or other casual uniforms, sometimes on the bridge that nothing (not even the lines of drying laundry) hid from view, sometimes on the riverbank, in the area immediately surrounding the modest craft in front of which passersby would, sometimes, stop to have a look or a little chat, probably in French or broken English, with one of these denizens of rivers and canals. Once I saw one of the three men, apparently alone on the boat, do a little dance with his hands in his pockets that looked to me like a jig, characteristically nautical and apparently intended less to warm himself up than to add what would have been just the right note to an imaginary production number.

When we no longer saw this boat and the small motorcycle that flanked it from our fourth floor balcony overlooking it on the quai, and realized that it, along with its three occupants, were gone, we very nearly grieved, since from then on, we would miss that charming, contagious vision of insouciance and joy.

◇

DANGER! LOOK OUT!

For a writer who like myself has for many years been happy to call himself a "realist," isn't it a ridiculous illusion to believe that you are fully grounded, well-anchored in the real, when your collection of realities is only piquant enough to cast a kind of spell and encourage you to forget that they are only special cases, far removed from making the entire body of reality more palatable? Those charming realities whose memory I enjoy fiddling around with and that serve as beautiful materials for me are nothing, in fact, but hypnotics: amiable diversions, they defuse my all too-real fear that it is not in their nature to genuinely reconcile me with the magma of stupidity and suffering that constitutes the world in which I live. When they show their true colors, they prove to be elitist, luxury realities, comparable to indigents who have been appropriately selected to have their feet washed by the pope in an edifying ceremony, or prisoners whose crime is politically fashionable enough for them to receive amnesty.

Believe me when I say that when I transcribe, I transcribe as faithfully as possible. But essentially, in much of my work these days, I am not very different from those academic artists who only paint or sculpt *beautiful* models and, probably, I am also something like the shrewd matador who accepts no other adversaries than those who, tailor-made, allow him to cut elegant figures without great risk.

It's hard for me not to be finicky and to dive in without hesitation, for I write less to confront evil and open other people's eyes to it than to deliver myself from my own personal hell and, starved for euphoria, seek most of all to strike a few matches to thwart my childhood terror of being trapped in the closet!

◇

COURTESAN REALITIES STOP SAD OR HAPPY BUT POETICALLY MANIPULABLE STOP LEAVE OTHER THANKLESS REALITIES ALONE STOP STILL OTHERS BITCHES NOT TO BE TOUCHED EVEN WITH A TEN FOOT POLE STOP YEARNING FOR REALITIES GIRLS TO TALK TO AND MAKE LOVE

$$\diamondsuit$$

Curious as you might be about everything that is being done or written about or said, there always comes a point—if you live long enough—when you no longer feel you belong to your time. Before, you were in it, or at least you had the illusion that you were. Now, you find that, in the domain that still might be considered your own, many things probably worthy of attention are being produced without you, and sometimes without your even being able to understand them. A conclusion you scoff at but that you must reluctantly, one day, come to terms with: you have lost your grip.

To no longer belong to one's time is to no longer be a part of life; it is to be already a part of death. Even if you can't be "among the vanguard," you should at least better understand—even if you disapprove of them—the current trends, realize (by putting yourself in their shoes) what's going on in the heads of your inheritors as they face circumstances totally different from those you faced, know how to interpret changes in fashion and how they affect cultural mores, try to determine the real motivations behind what's going on . . . Good plan, but highly daunting for a sociologist who doesn't know his own limits!

To grasp more immediately the meaning of what is being done or undone around me, to understand this "modern" that may very well exist—a patent revival—but that escapes me or seems to respond to decay because I am no longer directly affiliated with it, I would like to be able—using my intuition, as I have neither the time, nor even the desire, to study everything this era entails in minute detail—to extract what, for this part of the century, would be the essence of the ribbon that made Olympia seem more nude: the trait or detail of civilization that would symbolize and (incriminating evidence, symptom, identifying fingerprint) characterize the present era and subtly demonstrate what *this era* is, this particular phase of the human adventure, this phase endowed with its own truth, even if that truth completely baffles me!

◇

My father's friend was probably thinking of Le Pétomane, the famous flatulist whose vulgar act enjoyed great success towards the end of the last century when he spoke of the "posterior symphony" (or perhaps "variations" preceded by the same epithet) apropos of a fairly long motif performed by the bassoon in Richard Strauss' *Salomé*, which had recently premiered in Paris. For me, who had been brought to a performance of this lyrical drama probably without anyone knowing how inappropriate it was at my young age, the modulations of the bassoon evoked nothing scatological. I saw in them only—as in all of the music in that work, which was already unusual because by having only one act it strayed from the customs of grand opera—an expression of something I would have had great difficulty defining if I had tried and whose bizarre charm distinctly separated the work in question from those I had previously been acquainted with, having been initiated very early into the splendors of our National Academy of Music. Something that, had I possessed a richer and more extensive vocabulary and been more concerned with analysis, I could have called "modernism," understanding by what was being said around me that Salomé was a "modern" work, a product not only of our age but one whose very newness endowed it with originality.

A very different world to me than the one reading and theatre had until then allowed me to approach was revealed to me by the adaptation (faithful, I realized later on) of the play written in French by Oscar Wilde, a story that depicts, along with a kind of almeh, houri or Jewish bayadere who inspires male lust to the point of torture, a Herod whom I mistook for the Herod from the Massacre of the Innocents and a Yokanaan whom I didn't know was our St. John the Baptist called by his Hebrew name (which suggests rock splitting more than it does Canaan when it strikes my ear now, in my imagination).

A story that, thematically, resembles many stories told in the Scriptures but that diverges from them scandalously in the treatment of the material: an Oriental style imbued with magic and with precious, archaic touches that were missing from the edifying stories I had read or that were read to me; a warm, turbid atmosphere, weighed down by the inebriety aroused by Herod's incestuous desire and the erotic delirium that will possess Herodias's daughter when the head of the prisoner she had vainly attempted to seduce is delivered to her; the cruelty that seems to have been deliberately chosen as the dominant note of the action, which centers around the beheading of the saint but also involves the murderous stroke of the sword delivered by one of the princess' admirers almost immediately after his entrance and then, as the curtain falls, his barbarous execution that crushes him like a venomous insect under the soldiers' shields. A three-fold debauchery, since it simultaneously includes the quasi-sacrilegious intrusion of exoticism into an episode that adheres to the same kind of respectable hagiography as images of piety in which picturesque excess would seem inappropriate, an overt appeal to the louchest kind of sensuality, and sadistic recourses to a fascination with bloodshed. On top of that, the music was boldly dissonant, charged with strange emanations that commented on a drama whose text—an opera libretto I was only able to grasp in a general way, at first—would ultimately move me by the way in which the harshness of its storyline was united with the baroque, luxuriously insolent sumptuousness of the tenor. Warping, distortion, perversion that complicate the pleasure a work of art has to offer: these are—it seems to me now after many years during which a sort of decantation took place—the least deceptive (although very imprecise) terms I can use to characterize the form in which, tinted by a shade of purple with an eerie gleam, my first impression of modernity appeared, then only a hazy sensation I was unable to translate on even the most elementary theoretical level. No other opera I saw under the same circumstances, while it too may have distanced itself from what appeared to be the norm in that domain, would give me the same feeling: *The Jewels of the Madonna* by the Italian Ermanno Wolf-Ferrari, a verismo work about which, apart from its theme of a sacrilegious jewel theft, I only remember seeing, during the first act, in a trattoria scene, the French baritone Vanni Marcoux dressed as a Neapolitan pimp—in a crocodile mustache, elephant-footed pants and a gray bowler hat, I think—sing at the top of his lungs after having eaten, without any possibility of its being a trick, a huge plate of noodles or spaghetti, a performance that displayed an estimable concern for realism and considerable vocal skill but failed to inspire the imagination, much like the music (fairly conventional, I think) of that opera that, to my knowledge, has left no notable traces in the history of lyric theatre.

It was not, then, with that assuredly picturesque but inconsequential event but with *Salomé*, a new continent for my relatives almost as much as for myself, that I made this discovery: the glamour of modernity—a modernity which at that time was, of course, contemporary and which today would instead be called something like "kitsch" or "retro" (since the thing that, archetypically modern in another era, was considered in that era to be the latest style, is doomed by its very nature to go out of fashion and become the object of a slightly perverted, half-ironic, half-sentimental inclination towards something that, having become passé without yet having acquired the nobility of an antique, is attractive for the very reason of its obsolescence, the buffet in our childhood dining room, the contemporary jewelry worn by our first love, the automobile whose once-functional forms now seem absurdly stylized. Nevertheless, because I was too innocent when I accidentally drank Salomé's potion, as it were, I hadn't noticed that a door had cracked open on something important, and that the complex emotion I had experienced without being able or wanting to sort out its elements had awakened in me—barely an adolescent and blindly accepting the artistic and literary opinions of my parents—no desire to widen my horizon on that front. For the modern thing to inspire me, to fill me with enthusiasm or at the very least with curiosity, I would have to become a young man, eager to breathe an air that was his own and inspired to reject, in favor of other tastes, those that the education received from his father and mother had inculcated in him.

Like a twin of my accomplishments in the taboo domain of sex and as if my path towards the practice of love had had as a corollary or counterpart a burgeoning intimacy with the idea of death—love and death being as naturally coupled as two complementary colors that structure the life of a painting, along with being bound together in expressions (and this is perhaps what enticed me then) for things that are scandalous, practically obscene, to discuss without beating around the bush—the macabre, on the threshold of my adolescence, had cast its unseemly spell on me, which I endured not only in a more conscious but more deliberate and, I would say, more guilt-ridden way than I had the ominous allure of Salomé, that drama of love and death that had previously made such an impression upon me. A macabre that, along with other aesthetic revelations, Baudelaire's poem, *la Charogne*, had given me a taste of and whose macabre flavor only minds free of prejudices, in other words, "modern," seemed to appreciate. After being introduced to it, if I am not mistaken, by my older brother (who was planning on a career in the decorative arts at the time, a vocation from which he was hijacked by a marriage that would make him a banker and sheepish father to a large family), an image by Félicien Rops—a nude woman brutally confronted by a head with empty eye sockets and sardonically bared teeth—seemed to me, memory or fantasy, to occupy, like those melodramatic illustrations of a cheerful, colorful masquerade ball that suddenly turns tragic, a chosen place in that dubious zone where, from the distance of almost a lifetime, I see the coexistence of many things that pander to my tendencies when they speak of death, some openly, others in secret. A marginal zone where I have imagined guardroom or quat'z'arts orgies, trivial inheritors of Byronian feasts where punch was drunk out of skulls, that I was introduced to as much by Edgar Poe's tales of horror as by realist works such as Aristide Bruant's songs that featured traces of blood on the pavement and the guillotine, or even Jehan Rictus' bleak poems that were haunted by the threat of dying from hunger or cold, in between, on one side, the atrocious Chinese inventions dreamt up by Octave Mirbeau for Le Jardin des Supplices (a book that was forbidden to me for many years) and on the other, the dry and grating, almost funeral comedy of the Anglo-Saxon eccentrics who, more relevant and real than the circus clowns of my early childhood, produced corny and old-fashioned shows at the Alhambra music hall, an antiquated theatre near the Place de la République (rue de Malte, to be exact) that resembled Arab Granada in no shape or form.

When, from the heights that I have reached in what demographers call the age pyramid, I consider this taste for the macabre that I had for a time, it seems like the side effect of a childhood illness: too young to consider death a threat, wasn't I trying to prove that I was smart enough to dance with death and, defying propriety, to find some charm in its perfume? But I was not a little boy who took such minor liberties with bourgeois conventions to counterbalance his own innocence, but a young man hungry for elegance, combining a sham athletic style with quasi-feminine facial treatments, feverishly indulging in dances imported from the outer Atlantic, anglicizing himself by his choice of cigarettes and (as much as possible) by his dress, enjoying the intoxicating drinks and strongly spiced dishes served in American bars, a young man whose horizons had just recently been widened by love, who, on the brink of the roaring twenties, discovered the finest things of the expressly modern spirit that, partly out of snobbery and partly out of a real need to experience new worlds, he wished to make his own: the music, painting and poetry of the avant-garde, then in rebellion against the fin-de-siècle genre, its splenetic deliquescences and penchant for perverse façades.

Moved by the desire to participate, even if only as a witness, in the adventures of these three branches of the imaginary in the years before the war and out of a desire to find some beauty in a laboratory science such as chemistry, which I had foolishly chosen as my future professional field, as I had pursued "classical" studies and not those studies that were called "modern" because mathematics and science had a greater presence there and, in the scientific perspective dating from the last century, represented, like servants of Progress rather than of tradition, the modern par excellence, I subscribed to—a solution that straddled the fence—the aesthetic preached by the journal, *The New Spirit*: a technologizing modernism that, in awe of the material progress that the still young century had accomplished, made up the lion's share of the prevailing rationale, and sought its brand identity in the admiration for machines and other recent industrial achievements that, while they may have illustrated the era in spectacular fashion, characterized it only superficially; a modernism that was bloated and self-absorbed, proud to have played, by extolling the art of engineers, its part in the magnificent rise that the war we believed would be our last had accelerated rather than slowed but that, all things being equal, was as ingenuous as the modernisms had been that, in their day, exalted castles and armories or palaces and carriages as sublime indices of human genius' capacity for invention. That phase of my long struggle with ideas about invention is unquestionably the one that is most foreign to me today and it was, anyway, so brief that I can only consider it as being barely more than a false start. It seems to me, when I look back on it now, that it proved to be quite simplistic, deluding itself rather building on that "Progress" that became an opportune object of faith, even devotion, when it had to fill, by means of that belief in another providential authority, the absurd hole that had been hollowed out by the erosion of faith in an all-powerful god and the degradation of sovereign powers that had been imbued for so long with an almost sacred character by public consensus. Progress, the lay divinity that staggers nowadays under the weight of technological excess and whose salutary effect revolutionaries are the first to disavow, for, optimistic as their wagers on the future might be, they proceed as if it were impossible to improve the world without brutally forcing the natural course of things.

No longer believing in Progress as if it were Santa Claus, no longer thinking that preparatory stages are inevitably followed by better days and that my life, an uphill climb, therefore has, despite its brevity, some meaning, doubting the legitimacy of the Revolution (a high price to pay for what, if we have to overlook the concomitant losses, aren't necessarily gains), if it's true that I have made real progress as far as my judgment is concerned, how can I say what the disintegration of these ideas, which gradually have become my support without my realizing it, will reduce me to in my final years, by depriving me not only of a reason for hope but a precious axis of reference! In short, I've returned—less naive and enthusiastic, more disenchanted and skeptical, aggravated by fear and loathing of the violence that's spreading like wildfire—to the era of my troubled adolescence in which, less dazzled then by everything that assumed the color of the "modern" and gasping for air in a world whose laws condemn us to grow old and then to die, a fact I already understood (an anxiety that will soon bear down on my joys of being a lover bound to a unique and ephemeral object), I found no relief except when the imaginary was in full effect: conjoined with what gave form to my deepest feelings in image or song, the fictive transfiguration or dislocation of that oppressive interior, through prodigious and entirely new examples of poetry and art that were offered to me by people (Apollinaire and Picasso, among others) who seemed to me like prophets, if not pioneers. Beneath frivolous exteriors lay a dreamy adolescence that would not be contented by a vague amateurism and would soon be tormented by the demon of the inkwell, the desire to practice through writing a magic that, founded on my own desires, would be the only one likely to completely thrill me; an adolescence which, when I consider the magnitude of my current distress, I think the remedy in question, which I applied instinctively and haven't yet exhausted by my excessive thinking on the subject, made a happy one, although in those easier days, it granted itself the luxury of thinking the opposite.

Neither modernity (a smokescreen for those who, afraid of being seen as anachronistic as if that were some kind of evidence of their stupidity, would like to be the modern illustrations of what is definitively modern in their era but are generally only snobs well-trained in following whichever way the wind blows and so, in fact, follow on the heels of the people who couldn't give a damn about being modern or not being modern and who are the true pioneers), nor *modernity*, a false god, since we can only determine what was paramount to an era after the passage of time, but *eternity*—something that gives the resounding sensation of being somewhere other than in the temporal—that is what, after I had stopped worrying about being "in fashion," I was seeking in poetry and art whose time and space, the ossature of the world, seemed to belong neither to clocks nor meters but to speak to the view we would have of this world if, a fabulous eventuality I don't believe in, death were to liberate us from finitude's stranglehold. *Modernity, eternity*: it isn't simply an aesthetic taste for assonance, or even for wordplay, that brings me to draw a parallel between these two notions; I think that in fact there are no better words to describe the two poles I swung between until they ended up nearly merging with, or at the very least superimposing themselves upon, each other. A coincidence in no way paradoxical if we admit, as I do now, that an innovative work, or one that is not formally innovative but that seems to express the spirit of its age with acuity (to show, going deeper than external appearances, that it characterizes this particular era, one that will eventually pass away but that is alive for those who live in it and carries with it, as ours does, its own never-before-seen) is not only modern by definition but touches on the eternal, counting among those things that have the greatest chance for longevity (that remain intensely *present* despite the passage of time) precisely because of the immediately convincing way they capture and preserve the century's signature perfume, that thing that Baudelaire, applying the word to the fragile prestige of fashion and imbuing it with an entirely new color, called "modernity" in the days when Manet sketched his profile (in a top hat with a wide ribbon and his hair spilling over the top of his neck) and that, even though such a notion had only recently come into being, is the prerogative of no particular age, neither Atomic nor Stone, prehistory itself having hardly changed (from the Neolithic to the Paleolithic) without experiencing its own quarrels between the Ancients and the Moderns. And if we accept besides (a thought I am steered towards by the direction my predilections gradually took, I who abhorred realism when I was very young as if, too flat to allow me to prevail over my condition as a mere mortal, it would instead stick my nose in my own caca), if—setting aside music, which has its own incomparable qualities as a potion but can only occasionally put them into practice and, except through sung or psalmoded speech, does not use the quotidian tool of language—we admit that the impression of currency, of total relevance that we are given by this kind of work, even if its theme is extremely banal, creates this singular illusion: that, when we encounter the serendipitous transcription of a reality with a date and a place, that fictional but irrecusable indication of the present (or what was at one time the present) throws us outside of time, tears us from our habitual route at least for a moment, and hence deceives us (beats us at our own game, vanquishes us with our own army, catches us in our own trap, etc.). Certainly, for a writer or an artist, it is as absurd to claim to be modern as it is to claim to be classical, since it is only retrospectively, in consideration of the historical developments that have taken place, that anyone is able to say what was authentically modern about a certain era (what, in the limited but significant domain of the arts and letters, made that era so deeply innovative and defined it in relation to the ones that came before and after), and it is possible, besides, that the previous "modern," if it set a precedent, will be ultimately promoted to the "classical." But does an artist or writer lapse into a bogus modernism if he intends the fruit of his labor, less of a copyist or an interpreter than an inventor, to present itself as a window on the world of today for the minds of today and, the eruption of the immediate real giving form there to the imaginary, to assume as much immediacy—or life—for the person experiencing it as an event unfolding before his eyes there at that very moment—in short, speaking to us about today in the jargon of today, that this result of a contrivance be endowed, ugliness and beauty placed back-to-back, with that presence that, enigmatically, makes a work of art (experienced as a reality that reaches you directly and at exactly the right time) instantly force itself on you and appear to be specifically about you, a work whose pictorial inertia or aggregate of written words doesn't prevent it from engaging a myriad of viewers or readers in a sort of candid, unforgettable experience that temporarily eclipses everything else?

To write, form and content, in a perfectly "modern" way, not in order to (falling into line) participate in the latest trend or (assuming oneself to be a pioneer) strive to anticipate that trend, but to be real—to speak, outside of any exotic or folkloric fog, in a manner that fits, in the times to which I belong, within the framework of my mental as well as physical life—and thus be more likely to reach true presence, the correspondence that destroys all distance. . . I don't think there's anything more to say about that agenda, except perhaps that there's something idiotic about worrying about modernity these days, or getting worked up over questions of literature or art, since painting, sculpting, and writing seem too anodyne not to be anachronistic in this era of epidemic violence for which a weapon like a machine gun would be a more appropriate symbol than a fountain pen, a paintbrush or scissors, instruments that have no real teeth, however one may use them and that, besides, were invented not for someone proposing positive transformation (*changing life* instead of merely disseminating a new frisson) but for someone content with passively reflecting the world as it is. The machine gun, visibly "modern" with its clean lines of steel, polished and glistening. . . But for it to be something more than a toy gun, it must produce a real victory and not a deception. Is it reasonable, anyway, to apply the Baudelairean notion of modernity outside of its original context, which is aesthetics? The contingent, fugitive element it refers to is actually, according to the views expounded in *L'Art Romantique*, an ingredient of beauty, something that certainly makes up one part of the eternal but, reduced to that, would only be a dead abstraction. Modern activities such as watching television, working in a factory, driving to the country for the weekend, freely making love as a hetero- or homosexual, smoking marijuana, boldly breaking with routine by having one's head in the clouds or fighting against tyranny have, in themselves, only a tenuous relationship with modernity, a matter not of facts but of the impression that, subjectively, one gets of them, even if only by keeping one's eyes and ears open to the contemporary. What's more, it often happens that this modernity that is inconstant by definition and whose essence is itself often difficult to grasp, far from being centered around the aspects of modern life that one would expect, turns towards archaism (hence the popularity of Roman names during the French Revolution, Pre-Raphaelism and its ideals at the height of the period of industrial growth, the taste for "primitivism" that many artists found at the beginning of this century, the antiquity of the carved wooden idols in a work such as *The Rites of Spring* that was considered scandalous not so very long ago, and whose seemingly barbaric dissonances were a great musical revelation to me when I was twenty and thirsty for innovation, examples to which I am reluctant to add, since it is totally ridiculous, the current enthusiasm for the "retro," complete lunacy since, if becoming infatuated with the modern and following fashion trends is the norm, loving something solely because it used to be modern and is today passé, out of fashion, is an atrocious sophistication).

Not a quality belonging to objective facts (or the most conspicuous, and so to speak caricaturish traits of "the latest thing" in our contemporary world, condemned by social movements that work either secretly or in plain sight towards revolutionary acts that seek to avenge the past), not an attribute of positive realities that relate to sociology or history but rather a matter of sensibility, the artistic angle from which one understands the present as a need to seek beauty and youth elsewhere, in short, a question of state of mind, the one, at least, that the most perceptive of us seem to have and that, in time, has a chance to be recognized—in the external form it will have taken—as having been at the forefront and having contributed, promise for the future, to a significant stage in the evolution of ideas, that is how we might delineate a space outside of which this notion of modernity no longer has any reach, if it even still has meaning. Irreducible as much for its pure innovation in one field or another as for its trailblazing adherence to the most original things an era visibly has to offer (its design, its fashions, its major technological inventions, and the many other elements that contribute to drawing its spectacular profile), modernity is found more in the eye that sees than in the thing seen, in what one personally feels rather than what makes one feel its existence. And it can only be an entirely relative thing, not because every era has a modern that contradicts its past and because—like a costume so perfectly in fashion that it goes out of fashion even more quickly, or the super-chic, industrial-style building at the heart of Paris casually known as "Beaubourg" that, barely after it had been completed, made us think that, after only a short time, it seemed passé without having ever achieved the undeniable majesty of the artisanal masterpiece, the Eiffel Tower—an era's most obviously modern thing is the first thing about it that seems dated, but—a reservation that goes much further—because it is according to our current method of conceptualizing modernity (a concept tied to our current value system that, like one nail driving out another, will ultimately cede its place to a different system) that we judge today's illustration of it and what, for us, represents it in eras of the past.

If this is so, modernity is doubly transient, since we apply the matrix of a fluctuating notion to the constantly changing thing that it tries to understand. A modernity that is so fluid that we may think we have been tricked by an empty word when we try to determine what it means, but which we nevertheless know has a reality, at least within the limits of our immediate experience: a quality that, wherever it comes from, seems to be positively attached to certain things and certain people who are particularly representative, we think, of the era we are living in and the as yet unheard note it strikes. But, thinking of myself, neither a terrorist nor some other avant-garde militant, nor someone on the cutting edge of technology, nor even a *businessman** with stenographers and computers, I who, fluent in no foreign language, is the least cosmopolitan person alive and, even more embarrassingly, doesn't know how to drive or swim, and plays none of the sports or games that are vital credentials for a "man of culture" at the approach of the 21st century, I who am equally far from the vanguard when it comes to clothing, having barely evolved from the old days when I became a *fan** of Fred Astaire, my elder by around two years, and his Saville-Row wardrobe, and who, when it comes to love, professes certain libertine views but has not led a life in conformity with those views, thinking of myself—obviously of this era but who, making a mountain out of the minor chores of life in a society based on consumption, is behind the times in many respects—I wonder not without some concern where I can find my modernity, a quality to which, probably because I see it as a synonym for vitality, I attach importance. In the grand scheme of things, am I not rather right in thinking that, despite certain appearances to the contrary, I can in fact find one and that it must live— manifesting in no clearly legible sign on my body, or in my actions and gestures—in my deepest interior: my cruelly sharpened awareness of how hard it is to be an informed individual in these times, to be someone who thinks about things even the slightest little bit? If, despite all of this, I catch up with my century, it will be through a detour or, dare I say it, through the euphemism, *mal du siècle*, the opposite of an awestruck, quasi-unconditional adhesion to a century whose supposed grandeur could cancel out enough of its miseries for me, even if I didn't take to it like a duck to water, to at least feel proud to belong to it. This, in truth, is the entrance used by many who, although not necessarily despondent about or embittered by a daunting future, feel ill at ease in this century, a historical sequence they participate in at the very least as onlookers, and that includes their malaise (itself a changing form assumed by their misalignment or dissatisfaction) as one of its traits, a "modern" trait par excellence since it marks the singularity of an era in relation to the ones that came before it and, denouncing an inadequacy, tends to demonstrate that transformation is desirable in this world that is not the best of all possible worlds and that we have not yet succeeded in tailoring to fit us, assuming that we ever could! Mal du siècle: seen from the point of view of modernity, the current character of the eternal existential crisis, that constant plague, the mal of the century, of this century, would be—unless I am falling prey, as a side effect of memory loss, to the false intermingling of memories—what while scolding us, his young friends who were adherents of dadaism before we became surrealists, Max Jacob called "the spirit of nothingness," he who found in his Catholic faith, if not a panacea, at least a compass that somehow guided him and, at the same time, an anchor that protected him from these kinds of constant questions. But, whether or not a demoralizing demon revealed the end of his forked tail behind quite a few of the doors that opened in my head at that time, and whether or not I sometimes lent an ear to his bad advice, it's clear that these days, the ground is more fertile than ever for his denigrations.

The certainty that I am destined not only to die (no longer be conscious of anything) but to disappear *without a trace*, meaning that a day will come when no trace of myself will remain: that is the first thing I discover when I cast a panoramic glance across my mental landscape. What good will it do me—assuming I manage it—to leave a lasting mark on the world, if the laws of astrophysics destine our planet for extinction? What good is it anyway to strive, since whatever path I might have the opportunity to take will end in an absolute void, in always the same end, however I end up reaching it! This prospect of total annihilation that looms once and for all is obviously a dire one. But it concerns only the future, and, what's more, a distant future, quasi-imaginary, and that mitigates the awfulness of it somewhat. More immediate, though, is the muffled disquiet created by other weeds that have gradually invaded my internal soil, leaving me only a narrow space to plant what I would like to plant there.

It seems to me, first of all, that as mediocre as my understanding of Marx and Freud's ideas was, it led me to reject the idealism that had once exhilarated me, even during my periods of depression, as a mistake that stemmed from my benign and sheltered youth; an epiphany, to be sure, but one that included a disagreeable counterpart: our lyric impulses towards the sublime (white or black) are dashed when, after becoming aware of the enormous power of economics or sexuality, we understand ourselves as being manipulated from below more than directed from on high. Furthermore, the study and practice of ethnology, a science that hadn't yet become completely orthodox when I decided to make it my profession, had a severely demystifying effect on me: Western civilization is simply one civilization among others that are equally tenable, although none can be called Paradise, and it is useless to argue for the technical superiority of the West, as everything now tends to demonstrate the futility of the information and knowledge that Westerners have accumulated (which, by the way, they no longer have a monopoly on), undeniable progress but which works as much for evil—the capacity for destruction—as for good and, even though it may be accompanied by refined thinking, concerns only a limited domain, since no one can say, despite our societies' recent advances on issues such as the protection of children and the emancipation of women, that modern man, while his consciousness has developed over the course of centuries and his behaviors have evolved, is—in the depths of his body, which is on the whole more well-nourished and lavishly equipped with tools—a more intelligent and moral being than his predecessors in ancient, even prehistoric times. To each era, as to each country, its own forms of intelligence and morality. . . According to what criteria (we cannot even point to our increased lifespan, since death, even late in coming, is no less of a naked tragedy now than it ever was, or to the decrease in the daily murder rate per victim, since that artisanal mode of clearing the herd has been replaced by periodic massacre) do we establish a hierarchy and trace an ascending line that would transcribe an absolute Progress?

In the same reductive sense as the relativism that affects not only the Real and the True but also touches on the Beautiful (because tastes vary as much as cultures do, absolute aesthetic value cannot be decided by consensus), we now know that the most prestigious instruments we have—such as machines and articulated language, which seem to give the measure of our transcendence in relation to all other living beings—are served by us at the same time as they serve us: we must consume what industry produces rather than produce only what we need or would like to consume and—another violation of the illusions of sovereignty that privately feed each and every one of us—the system of signs that is our means of expression not only becomes, through the intervention of the general press (printed or oral), the tool of the most cretinous kind of propaganda but, as it imposes its structures on us, influences everything we think, say, or write, leading us around by the nose while each and every one of us could be using it as a weapon to affirm our individuality and defy every external constraint. A relativism that is still very far from being unanimously shared, but that makes its official entrance in the historical period called "modern times," which my high school curriculum placed just after the "Middle Ages" and before the "contemporary era" (an odd label, since it was said to begin with the French Revolution), modern times that were not yet Chaplinian and even less Sartrean and which customarily date from the fall of the Byzantine Empire but in fact only began to rise with the discovery of America (first thought to be the Indies but soon recognized to be the "New World"), a discovery that, along with other adventurous sailings, overturned the foundations of geography and—with the spectacle of rich, unknown empires found beyond the sea on that land that, at first curling up in a ball, would soon cease to be the center of the world—the type of almost cloistered absolute that Christianity had represented for so long, modern times whose beginnings also saw the development of serious and direct challenges to the authority of the Church: the invention of the printing press, through which the Bible passed in some way into the public domain and, with the creation of the idea of *free inquiry*, the spiritual revolution called the Reformation. A relativism that emerges, tutelary truths having been struck a harsh blow, as soon as the guaranteed tradition of security cedes to the contingencies of the modern in which, despite all the lessons I have learned and thinking I have accomplished, I am so profoundly steeped that I experience, a reaction that isn't exactly rooted in ideology but caused instead by the lack of a solid means of support, a feeling of uncertainty such that, doubting my legitimacy as well as my judgment, I don't even dare consider myself the owner of anything that I handle less directly than the clothes I am wearing, my small collection of writing instruments (in particular, a fountain pen, ballpoint pen and mechanical pencil), the notebooks that I write by hand, or the books that surround me: luckily, as for the bulk of what I have at my disposal, although in part a salary for some of the work I've completed in my two chosen fields, I have (as far as I see it) a few usufructs, and nothing more; and if I jealously cling to them, as much, perhaps, as a bourgeois miser, I am not unaware that I do so with the egotism of a dog attached to his bone, and not because I believe them to be a natural, unquestionable prerogative.

Nevertheless, if in addition to the skepticism that the leftists of my generation were forced to accept regarding the blessings that revolution might bring, I feel all of this so strongly, as a response to the truths that cannot be denied by any man of our era who is even slightly curious or reflective, can I really speak about my modernity, I who endure what I call the *mal du siècle* as I would endure a toothache, seasickness, or a disease? To be authentically "modern," shouldn't I confine myself to recognizing those bitter truths (first the knowledge, of which atheism convinced at least some Westerners, that death is a passage into nothingness and that, if the ephemerality of the modern holds so much charm for so many of us, it's because of the awareness of our own ephemerality), not limit myself to being a knowledgeable man who harbors no illusions but present myself as being somewhat at ease and somewhat free, to put on a brave face, like a Baudelarian dandy, would, instead of refusing the shelter of humor's umbrella and standing out in the rain, in short, not conform to the century any more than the whipping top conforms to the whip or the victim to the executioner?

Combatting accepted ideas, taking liberties with norms as well as with standard morality: it is this casual rejection of old-fashioned notions that still have clout, and not the discriminating intellectual's despondent attitude or honest grief about the bleak news stories reported daily through the media of the various gadgets whose contented acceptance the new age proposes to us that, logically, responds to modernity. A critical attitude, at least implicitly. And yet, in my area of expertise, shouldn't a deeply heterodox mind prevail? To be a real "modern"—neither someone who lags behind, nor a simple follower, but one of those visionaries who creates the era in his own way, contributes to its moving towards something other than our current understanding of what previous eras seem to have exemplified—we must in fact be ahead of it and hence against it to some degree, approaching it if not head-on at least from behind, if not directly at least indirectly, in complete innocence, even, investigating our way of living as members of a human society that maintains its own habits and history, and committing ourselves (without heaviness and without necessarily becoming enraged) to that task that at a minimum is subversive by definition, instead of abandoning oneself to the facilities of fashion or behaving like a misanthrope who only dwells upon his own disgust. I won't deny myself the pleasure of indulging in a phrase I find intoxicating, even if I use it to argue the contrary when I say that modernity is not a matter of striving to prove that the era fits you like a glove, but demands instead that you keep your distance from it, otherwise there's no possible way for you to channel your efforts towards renovation. In that sense, modernity would be the privilege of a few who, detached on the whole from their contemporaries, are in the more or less inopportune position of being pioneers but, because they do not belong to an established body devoted to a cult of the modern for the modern, do not qualify as "avant-garde" and hence become the subject of one of the most widespread of those *military metaphors* that were denounced by Baudelaire as so dear to the French mind.

Modernity, then, that instead of a flag would be the ribbon that, without even knowing it, certain people wear around their hats. A modernity that, in the end, slips between your fingers in every respect: relative, because it only exists in relation to what is considered to be old-fashioned according to ideas that never stop changing, and hence is too radically uncertain (the opposite of the immeasurable Absolute that belongs to the essential and not the contingent) for any reassuring cult to be devoted to it; fleeting, given that time passes so quickly that a new modern always looms behind the one that we believe we have grasped; changing even on an individual level since, in order to be one hundred percent modern, one must also be modern in relationship to oneself and, while brooding on and surrendering to habit, remain constantly on the alert; polymorphic, since there are many ways to resist conformity and open up pathways towards the future simply by flatly rejecting (consciously or unconsciously) what is ordinarily accepted; opposed to any criteria other than negative criteria, so it can only be characterized as an unprecedented means of dissent, the only common element of its various reincarnations. A modernity that, we cannot stress this enough, is not directly based on the modern world (does not model itself on its objective traits) but on the nearly unprecedented personal reactions of those who find themselves immersed in its ensemble of things, events and ideas. Reactions that, for those concerned, will lead to behaviors that are infractions or exceptions to the rule (if not categorical, at least establishing shifts away from it), disturbing what is normally acceptable in one way or another, and so these nonconformists will be readily seen as madmen, perverts, corruptors or charlatans, that is to say, degenerates or practical jokers who only escape the fate of a psychiatric hospital or prison camp in countries that are branded by a certain cultural liberalism. If it is no longer possible to be truly scandalous in countries without an authoritarian State philosophy that abruptly dictates questions of orthodoxy or heterodoxy or where, on the contrary, the terrible mess that's been made of things engenders an agnosticism in many that leads them to reject all doctrines back-to-back, along with the fact that compared to the enormous scandals currently disgracing our world, smaller, less lethal scandals seem ludicrous, we understand that in less troubled times innovations such as, for example, the music of Wagner (who can claim Richard Strauss as one of his inheritors) or Impressionist painting (including Édouard Manet, among others) were able to create an uproar: the authentically modern work appeared as a challenge to common sense, a tasteless joke, even an attack on morality, and so it isn't surprising that what we see emerging today seems even more like a pathetic pretension, an obscene striptease or a thumbing of the nose that, screwing with the sublimity of high art, is just as sacrilegious as the ironic addition of a thin mustache on the upper lip of *Joconde* (Marcel Duchamp, a.k.a. Rrose Sélavy, *delineavit*).

Relativism. Skepticism of sacrosanct foundations. Demystification. Ambiguity towards the world we live in, which we rebuff because of its crippling vices but to which we remain attached the instant its gods are slain because it is our only reality and nothing, except for that thing that lives outside of us but is as obvious and familiar as a friend, can—without deception—fascinate us, certainly not in its entirety but at least in certain pieces of what our business with it offers us. The opposite of Christ, deaf to the Tempter who, to divert him from his eternal mission, invited him to reign over the actual world whose splendors he revealed to him in a panoramic vision (the same corrupt world that Salome's Yokanaan oppresses with his curse), modern man is—in the archaic sense of the term—a *mondain* who, no longer able to rely on any religion (including the cult of reason, divinity of the state school variety, and the bust of the Republic), seeks to base his wealth on what the world dispenses to him according to its ups and downs. Superficial, of course, and questionable in that respect, but how preferable to the false profundity of the apparently global understanding that provides a questionable creed! A positivist line if you like, but a positivism that erects no dogmatic framework, as it is understood that our definitive knowledge of science is far weaker than our ignorance and that, in order for it to be science, the realism that all science involves demands that it perpetually call its accepted and tireless research into question, and never rest on its laurels. A positivism that doesn't weigh itself down, that does not congeal into doctrine but remains pure non-belief and is so unconstrained that, although the enemy of the illusion it falsifies, it considers neither desires nor dreams to be weeds and does not restrict the flowering of the imagination, however baroque it may be. And so there is, if not in every modern artisan, at least in the small number of them who seem to have been possessed by the mal de siècle in an exemplary way, an undeniable diabolism, if to become deliberately attached to the surfaces of things (today's surfaces, without yesterday's wrinkles or tomorrow's costumes), and build evanescent architectures upon them, is to turn away from the Absolute—a.k.a., God—and, unabashedly sinning against the serious mind, position themselves against him as rebellious angels.

Finding heaven on earth, conferring eternity upon a moment lived in complete lucidity, these are the joys that the modern demon of negation occasionally grants to someone who, refusing to pull the wool over his eyes, relies only on the present—the direct, the immediate, the without-memory or anticipation—and is perhaps fulfilled only by what the dazzling sensation of its presence imposes upon him, outside of any reasoning as well as any plan—not the presence of whatever normally imperceptible thing suddenly manifests visibly, but the presence of that very appearance that requires nothing more than its own radiance to strike us with awe. I don't think it is idle verbal coquetry to speak of the "beauty of the devil" in regard to these slices of the present that, luring us to vertigo, are not only presence itself—undisguised bait, the fresh meat of the here and now—but of an impossible duration that affects us even more deeply than we realize. Besides, for us to speculate that the devil reveals a glimpse of his horns in that, it is enough to imagine the paradox, even of the sin embodied—flashes in the pan that are no less powerful for it—by these types of gifts: doesn't understanding that they disappear almost as quickly as they were offered to us, and then privileging them accordingly, demonstrate the guilt-ridden futility of lovers of the ephemeral, as serious and noble as our emotions may have seemed to us when those rare fortunes appeared?

There's nothing contradictory about maintaining a resolutely irrational *yes* (too spontaneous and free to be subject to any logic) without relinquishing the *no* imposed by the rational, for that *yes* is pronounced without the slightest credulity and, if the negation remains, it is like a desert where mirages appear that we know are only grafts, or the most aleatory methods used by the mind to process reality in its untamed state. An irony that consists in condescending—not without a morbid internal sneer—to the sad truths we know only too well and refusing, despite the facts that knowledge and experience have dictated to us, to reject, in devotion to reason, the poetry that life has to offer (or allow) us despite its terrible flaws, returning to the pious imitation of the Christian who, from the moment of his baptism, renounces Satan, his works and pomps. Aren't the modern and the sinful intimately connected, besides? On the one hand, sin, from the perspective of the Catholic faith, is "modern" in the sense that it constitutes a non-alignment, a violation of the Law, a breach of the divine plan by an independent arbitrator; on the other hand, if the "modern" is thought to be more urban than rural, it may be because it accommodates folklore's old-fashioned charm even less than it does religion (a traditional system aimed at disguising the hideous reality of death), but it is also because the big city, the place where fashions are created and technology displays its latest developments, represents the ultimate place of corruption, since as a rule it is there where luxuries of every genre flourish— great white peacocks in the gardens of Herod the tetrarch—and where all kinds of *Salomés*—some in flesh and blood, others who bewitch us with ideas as shiny as gold coins—perform their dances of the seven veils or other, more insidious schemes.

Priest of no cult, either religious or political, but a magician (who inspires us to master rather than serve a god, to use what can be handled to touch what can't be grasped, to bet not on the anonymous generality but on the detail that may be no wider than a hair's breadth but that delivers, pays off instantly, right now, instead of waiting for a future reward), a *thief of fire* (without Promethean furor but gluttonous, hungry for pirate swag), impious (as his activity is opposed, whether he likes it or not, to outdated beliefs and represents in itself a kind of sin in the eyes of puritans who are exclusively concerned with useful actions), idolatry (that places his art above all else, although he no more believes in "art for art's sake" than he does any other religion), solitary (given his role as visionary), the artist or writer who, more likely than the rest of the people in his profession to be deemed "modern" because he is the most radical, has only a slim chance of escaping being damned—as a maverick, an outcast, or even a black sheep—or of receiving anything more than dubious recognition; hence Picasso, crowned by glory with an incomparable halo whose rays, for many philistines, were tinged with evil.

Pity for our errors pity for our sins, wrote Apollinaire, probably not really believing that very much but feeling a need to make a plea for himself and those who were on his side. . . Even so, according to everything that he gave me to read and know about him, it doesn't seem that the radiant and Dionysian Apollinaire, who was one of the great moderns of my adult life and almost a god to me, could be classified as one of the accursed, even though he was very early and unfortunately struck down by fate. Despite the sadness that was wholeheartedly voiced in the haunting timbre of his lines, there was nothing dark or negative about that poet, whom Max Jacob praised in the old days for what he called his "milky abundance" and who, even in his humor, only demonstrated baroque fantasy and a mind inclined towards mystification allied with solid common sense. Besides, isn't it a mistake, while theorizing modernity as it currently seems to appear, to refer to someone whom death silenced so long ago, and whose centennial was recently celebrated, perhaps less sumptuously than it should have been but with respect and admiration nevertheless? Besides this dubious example, there is clearly a flagrant anachronism in this appeal to the evidence of a "modern" that existed a good half-dozen decades ago and from which certain poems appear in the school books of today, for which I will be found guilty, oblivious to the passage of time and happy, incidentally, to draw on an authority who was no less minor in the field of literature than Picasso was in the field of art. By taking this route, I will then have stacked the deck twice, a harmless trick that is probably not the only one surreptitiously created by my panicked fear caused by having surpassed the age at which a person has the right to call himself "modern" and, to ward off that fear, my unspoken desire to create a bespoke modernity for myself, a modernity as I imagine it and whose scrutiny might appease my anxiety as much as a theorem that adequately proves my modernity—in other words, YOUTH—and reaches the triumphant conclusion of Q.E.D.

. . . So there!

Having said all that, not in an academically organized argument but an accumulation of almost off-the-cuff remarks, modernity—about which I'm still tempted to argue, parodying

Oscar Wilde's sentence, "There are as many Hamlets as there are melancholies," that for every moment in history there exist an equal number of forms clad in the mal du siècle—that modernity I will have worried myself sick over and that has made me equivocate so terribly, get so muddled up that, sardonically, I could easily call it *mudernity [merdonité]*,[1] (a variant more fitting than the too far-fetched *mets-d'or-nité*) [dishes of gold], isn't it, from wherever you stand, a dilettante's preoccupation that would be better off stowed away in a prop warehouse somewhere when an era, such as our own increasingly oppressive and bloody one, has become so atrocious that—for the people who live in it, especially those who like me once ingenuously bet on the future they saw dawning in the East—"modern" has come to designate not something you would like to sink your teeth into, but something that sinks its teeth into you? It's a scintillating idea, that the poet who picked those *fleurs du mal* so imbued with sin that they broke the law would be cast in the same every-inch-an-artist mold as the one he attributed to dandyism . . . A stimulating but obsolete notion that I will no longer dwell upon, modernity— off-limits in these loathsome times where such a way of seeing proves to be the passé luxury of a fashion or a false note that wounds the ear, when it would be crazy to interpret the world according to that sort of model (the present and its enchantments, the uninspired past), a world that our massive information systems prove is decidedly charged with horror and inspires more disgust than astonishment—hasn't it, an affront to its very name, ceased to be modern?

---

1. See introduction: the slightly more anodyne alternative given here lacks the full scope of the original.

◇

The past, pierced by so many memory holes that a considerable part of my time is spent scheming (hedging after making a frontal, surprise attack, letting it go for a while before returning to it in full force, performing every roundabout trick imaginable) while trying to remember the name or the word that I find—a lugubrious sign—has sunk like a stone.

The present, more and more resistant to any rapacious grasp of it, so thick are the veils that intervene, screening the gaze that becomes dull and scattered instead of coming into focus, the dampened or discordant ear, the mind a swimmer propelling himself through a gelatinous mass.

The future, so obscured by the worries that besiege us and so brief from this point on that I make only modest, short-term plans (the furthest from today: in two months, going to see and hear a Monteverdi work that the Paris Opera has scheduled for the first part of its 1978 season).

The past in ruins, the present in disarray, the future in tatters: little remains for me apart from the clear awareness of this disaster, catastrophic but minor compared to the one that has begun to break apart the world, in which many of us have lived foolishly believing that the men of our era would at least ensure that it would survive.

$\diamond$

Demolished, razed,
desolate, tormented,
demoralized!

Frayed rafts,
drafts astray,
winds dying away.

◇

Losing his grip, no longer able to handle the suspense and thinking that, if it goes on like this, it won't be he who dies but someone who no longer resembles him, one night in that season of the year when it seems as if the days are refusing to end he makes, by himself, the great leap that tears him from himself.

◇

Color of the moon, of lymph or linen (except for the blush of her mouth and its barely perceptible incarnation on her cheeks) yet neither dreamy nor splenetic, lazily spread out on her finely brocaded bedcover, Olympia—full of only serenely predatory thoughts, perhaps—seems all the more limpid and pale with a pitch-black braid at her irreverent throat. . .

◇

Fine-tune the statue,
enumerate it: blazons.

Or else?

Nameless
the other thing I could do by stringing out words
sleep
—that's the trouble—
told me about one, wilder,
but would not name it
either in riddles
or in rebus or in code.

$\diamondsuit$

Who only cries silently but raises his voice over the slightest thing.

Who tries to bandage his irreparable original wound with words.

Who never lowers the mask, a man who shaped language that others have shaped.

Who bears solitude badly but is only slightly more comfortable in the company of others.

Who is wary of drugs, alcohol and black coffee, since they only aggravate his turmoil.

Who usually returns disappointed from the casual meal he had looked forward to as if it were a party, and blames himself for not having been up to it.

Who claims to be as marginal as poetry, but would like to make at least slightly political work and, without going any further, to become a captivating storyteller instead of only talking about himself.

Who, to escape, forages in the depths of himself.

Who, while trying to treat his depression, too naively confuses diagnosis with therapy.

Who no longer expects a cure for his obsessiveness, since if it were curable, he would already be cured.

Who does not hope for any great happiness, for fear of being thwarted by bad luck.

Who weaves between these three images: the one others create for him, the one he creates for himself, and the one he thinks he sees in the mirror.

Who isn't vain until he thinks he's modest.

Who doesn't want to be decorated and doesn't want to pride himself on that refusal: internal decoration would be just as stupid as the Legion of Honor.

Who, while not a masochist, still listens to the news.

Who senses, at a planetary level, the extinction of the values he once championed as a calamity that makes the prospect of his own extinction even more calamitous.

Who, hopes dashed and face-to-face with bitter melancholy, often unleashes his bile in black humor's vinegar form.

Who, waking every morning in a panic, must steel himself from head to toe against the approaching day.

Who, when alarmed, busies himself and who, when busy, is alarmed.

Who, when he looks deeply within himself, feels horror rising to his throat.

Who suffers anticipatory regret, not knowing what ignominies his shortcomings might cause him to commit.

Whose lair is a body that's become a hovel, or at best, an abandoned ballroom.

Who watches his canine acolyte grow old as if he were looking in a mirror.

Who knows he is an animal but, in writing, would like to claim otherwise.

Who, when his eye is riveted to a chain of words, is protected from the sight, out of frame, of death's unchaining.

Who would be a common junkie if his downward spiral weren't concretized into a consumable product by that *other*, the potential reader.

Who dislikes who he is, but likes to be able to say that he is.

Who, when he disguises himself in anatomical diagrams, strives to arrange his entrails in elegant rinceaux.

Who sometimes reproaches himself for not dying of his own song, like Hoffmann's Antonia or the legendary swan.

Who—perhaps a moral prejudice—prefers the musical reel to the reel caused by fermented drink.

Who loves to bitch about art, like an invalid ranting against his asylum.

Who goes line-to-line as others go door-to-door.

Who, as a poet, desperately tries to deny the absurdity of the way everything is touched by death.

Who, without claiming glory or permanence, seeks his nectar of immortality in the regrettably intermittent flow of writing.

Who thinks the world of his obsessions, however less vital they may be than eating, or drinking, or air.

Who cheers every time he cashes his royalty check, as if he found in it a justification.

Who, despite his aversion to trickery, leaves no stone unturned to find the trick.

Who plays with dice he knows are loaded but, after losing, is shocked and dismayed that he was robbed.

Who, having neither given life nor taken it away, has not spun the wheel of the world.

Who deplores being repulsed by politics, a necessary thing, since the fate of mankind depends on it.

Who, since the socialist framework has thoroughly missed the boat of LIBERTY, wonders if we should work to change our strategy or turn the page.

For whom a materially soft life has allowed plenty of moral luxuries!

Whose defiance of rock-solid certainties runs the risk of building over rotten foundations.

Who often thinks he is an island, but doesn't know exactly which Spartan he is.

Who speaks badly of himself to speak badly of others indirectly.

Who considers existence ridiculous without being able to laugh at it.

Who swings between being anxious wakefulness and stagnant drowsiness.

Who, hardly alone and still having some recourses at his disposal (literary work, Dogmatil, warmer and longer baths that are warmer and longer than necessary, opera, gallery visits, constitutionals, etc.), should obviously stop complaining.

Who is more and more ashamed of his ineptitude in this tour de force: remaining even-tempered in all circumstances.

Who is seized with fear like a dog who senses death in the house.

Who, too aware of what those terms denote, hesitates before using the expressions, "Sorry," or "Regrets."

For whom words become dead letters when things go wrong.

Who doesn't understand why human beings, already under the most terrible kind of spell, so often seem to enjoy making things worse.

Who bets on the milligram that might tip the scales towards a moment of happiness.

Who can't eliminate his contradictions without erasing himself.

Who is loath to accept the lowly quidam instead of the prized mikado.

Who has nothing left ahead of him but lying down—as if on a quilted mattress—next to so many friends who also could not be protected.

Who tries to finish this book just as his own life and the civilization to which he belongs are coming to an end.

For whom the moment of beauty comes at a greater and greater price, like the way gold rises on the Exchange when catastrophe looms.

Who, even though he can dress himself up, knows he has become a horrifying old man.

Who—passionately—wishes for the miracle-moment, but ignores the art of tasting the sweetness of the possible moment.

Who, even though he would need ropes, cables, even steel tethers, clings to just fifty centimeters of ribbon!

Who, without being prouder for it, will not have made peace.

Who bears no grievance against his father and mother, except that giving him life was a death sentence.

Who is devoted to this odd alchemy: transforming his unshed tears into ink, after they've become sludge and nausea inside of him.

Who knows all too well that "I" is not *an other.*

◇

The opposite of naked *Olympia*, the corseted and skirted *Nana* has beside her neither a servant of another race nor an animal of another species to honor her but only—shown seated and in profile on the right side of the painting—a middle-aged bourgeois in a top hat, black suit and white dickey, a john who seems to be sizing up the woman-object just as the work itself will be judged by the amateur.

Olympia, Nana: hardly femmes fatales, but pleasure manufacturers, as certain people make weapons and others, chocolate.

While in the past, more arrogant and more innocently convinced that poetic writing is intrinsically valuable and requires
nothing from the outside to justify the decision to create it, I
didn't care about having a large audience or worry about how I
would be judged by posterity, my doubts have grown to such a
degree that, without really owning up to this desire that may
very well stem from an absurd vanity, I sometimes find myself
longing for a best-seller.

Of course, I'm not trying to find some proof of the quality
of my work by that measure, as the reception given to books is
no kind of criteria in that respect and I do not believe that to be
recognized necessarily means to be understood, followed, to
wield any power or, in this case, to wield it over a great number
of people. But, at least in those moments when all confidence
abandons me, I think that presenting a work that interests only
a small number of supposedly "informed" people makes no
sense. What a sad little pipe dream it would be, in fact, were it
not to have—the only way, as serious is its content may be, to
escape insignificance or even, I'd go so far as to say, to exist—an
impact, not only on the few people who are open to that luxury
and already agree with me, but an anonymous group of my peers
who are then convinced of something that, alongside of their
various concerns, asserts its significance in relation to realities

that are real enough for a large number of human beings to be concerned about them!

What, in short, torments me, without yielding to an opportunism I find vulgar and that I would only practice awkwardly, besides, is the stupid but disarming notion that a work remains null and void if its legitimacy isn't demonstrated not only by the fact that it resists the waves of the quotidian tide better than a castle in the sand in the minds of people who already agree, but that it has the same effect on a group of people with all kinds of opinions whose numbers are large, that *sine qua non*, that shopkeeper's measure, the statistic, causing the crudest possible blocks of reality to take shape, a confirmation without a response, like—in this case—the voting block that decides a literary success.

(Defeatist words, whispered in my ear by the perfidious angel or devil's advocate whom my mind will continue to harbor until it is cleared by senility's vacuum!)

◇

How to wrap around the necks of things—around at least some of the things I trade in—the ribbon that would make them, for myself as much as for the people to whom I speak about them, as present, pressing, as Manet's *Olympia* and her throat striped black? A precious ribbon which, forgetting that it's only a frill embellished by a knot, a kind of shoelace, I would like to have at my disposal and create—safeguard against drowning—the light but supportive belt of cork that its circular embrace evokes. . . A ribbon, however, examining its painted image more closely—a narrow ligature cinching a neck that sits squarely atop its shoulders—I should instead classify in the same shadowy family as the victim's garrotte or the hangman's noose!

Placing a grain of salt on a bird's tail to catch it, tying the ribbon—or performing the trick—that would provide, almost instantly, the bliss of investing something that affects consciousness with poetic power: operations that only make sense in non-sense, for what good is a prize that can only be awarded when, the prey already in our hand that needs only to grasp it before it flies away, the problem to solve has already been solved?

Standing on the edge of a platform so crowded that right when the train enters the station I will be thrown on the rails.

The thin plank on which, when pushed from behind, I have only several meters to cross before falling into the sea.

Always easy to fix until now, the engine that, this time, cannot be repaired or replaced.

The garment I will wear for the first time, but won't have the time to get used to.

The date whom, having vanished forever, I will leave in the lurch without being able to apologize.

The bottle I will have to leave, half-full, on the table.

The day I sensed that my luck had run out, and that I was destined to lose on every table.

Neither gulf nor summit, the void into which, anchor or feather, I am plunged.

Too late to help me, the epiphany that will teach me just what Olympia's ribbon means.

Precise object of dread: the page that I will leave unfinished— and yet that is my wish, for I hope that I can work (to assert myself there) until my final breath.

Sometimes and especially now, in these times that lead us to consult oracles and astrologers because our worries about the future of the world are so great, I think of the young woman I saw one night in Cologne not so many years ago who, staggering down the sidewalk in a gait somewhere between running and falling, with pauses followed by fresh, abrupt starts, pounded her two fists on the ground-floor windows that she passed on the way. Was she drunk or high? Or so desperate that she was begging for help from anywhere she could get it? Unless she was just rebellious, determined to disturb the peace of law-abiding citizens spending their evenings in intimate quiet. . .

Whatever had caused the frenzy of this girl, whom I glimpsed only briefly but whose fragile and unstable silhouette lacked neither grace nor juvenile elegance, it was painful—for a foreigner such as myself, eating dinner with my family in a suitably vetted restaurant—to think that somewhere outside, this lost soul was knocking on windows not knowing where to turn, to which saint or devil, to avoid being alone with her torment.

Seeing the perfect happiness of the young child whom he had brought to the circus to introduce him to its celebrations, he had a half-tender, half-lacerating feeling and when, at one point while watching an act of flying acrobats in sequined leotards the boy's sweet face broke into complete rapture, he struggled not to burst into tears, thinking of this mockery: that his young, naïve companion would one day probably become like him, a man cured of any hope of happiness.

A scene of this kind might just as easily have taken place in a zoo, either while watching a bear stand up on its back legs, or a group of monkeys nimbly executing their gambols, or an elephant delicately picking up a dinner roll with the end of his trunk, or else in the street, during the crossing of a slow cortège of republican guards on horseback.

◇

"I don't want to kill you!" Then, almost as if in an aside, and in a less violent tone, despite its implicit aggressiveness: ". . . Not at the moment." To which I respond, wanting simply to say that I couldn't possibly imagine being the victim of an attack: "I haven't the slightest idea," words that elicit from the other a cold conclusive, "There it is," indicating that the matter—if a dispute in fact had occurred—was resolved, or that the case—if there was one—was closed.

This took place in the métro, in first class. My interlocutor and I were sitting back to back, he on a banquette, next to no one, and I on a jump seat. He, probably in his mid-thirties, had very dark hair, a pale face, and was clean-shaven, apart from thick sideburns that ran down to the middle of his ears; an undoubtedly tall young man (hence his quiet felling), and definitely handsome, albeit a bit coarse. Was he drunk? Or was he some kind of trickster, hoping to frighten the old man that I am? I'll never know, particularly because, just after this short conversation, I had to leave our car to change trains.

I note only that at the moment when he called out to me, this man whose back had been turned to me was reading the newspaper, *Le Monde*. In that edition—I knew this because I had the same paper in my hands one or two hours earlier—an article had been devoted to the arrest, in an apartment in the 5th arrondissement, of five young Germans suspected of having been connected to the Baader-Meinhof Group and the Red Army. The man who had spoken to me was certainly not a terrorist, but I wonder if, reading the article in question, his thoughts had perhaps turned sympathetic to their ways: kidnapping, hostage-taking, indiscriminate murder or, by whatever route it might take, rupture with the basic rules that protect bourgeois life.

◇

Cutting the hands, cutting the feet, even cutting the ears or nose can be performed without it being fatal. But not cutting the throat, chopping the relatively slender stalk that connects the head to the torso. The throat's ornament, then, is especially poignant—touching on an innocent part of the body, any radical mutilation of which will cost the victim her life—and even more so if, a ribbon made of supple fabric and not a necklace of hard mineral elements, it is intended to hide and discreetly repair a light but cruel wound that cut into that neck.

Isn't it to hide (disguise) and, if possible, heal (by overtaking it) the canker that eats away at my spirit and that, literally, is the *unspeakable*—which I wouldn't be able to articulate even if I knew how, since to admit that I am so completely lacking in faith would be a complete abdication, morally—that I so often act as if, repelled by the stench of the abominable swamp that is the unspeakable, my only goal were to turn writing's ribbon into a trap for the *ineffable*?

◇

It was, I believe, an elegant pimp named Linda de Castillon who, towards the end of the last century, murdered Marie Aguettant, a courtesan. It was not, as far as I know, a sadistic crime à la Jack the Ripper (although it was, I think, a throat-cutting and not a relatively clean strangulation), not a fatal gesture dictated by some kind of passionate rage but, in the soft warmth of a bedroom belonging to a popular courtesan, an aggression prosaically motivated by the desire to steal the jewelry or other treasures belonging to the victim, a romanceless and so to speak functional murder that led its author to the guillotine.

Was it by pulling a cord, like someone handling an old-style toilet flush or firing a cannon, or by pressing a modern button that the executioner, dressed all in black—perhaps in a frock coat and bowler if not a stovepipe, as that ceremonial headgear was called for many years—dropped the guillotine blade on the bare neck of the condemned man, whom I imagine having a head of beautiful raven-black hair and a crocodile mustache on a face with the bluish features of a gypsy or rasta, this condemned man who, over the course of a brief but undoubtedly rocky career that ended with Marie Aguettant to both of their misfortunes, had seduced—we might imagine—many women with his swaggering airs and his supple, feline gait, not the rolling gait of that formerly famous variety of waltz (later, though, since it dated from the beginning of this century)?

When Linda de Castillon, or the man we presume to be him, was punished for having treated a mistress as if her profession called for death as much as for love, capital executions were public and, it seems, as attractive to the world of high society as they were for the underworld. And so, it is not outlandish to think that many of the ladies of the evening whom he made rise to the seventh heaven witnessed his severed head fall into the wicker basket.

Closer to the Saint-Lazare railway station and its bluish smoke than the Dead Sea and its waters overloaded with salt, not the head of John the Baptist bleeding on a silver plate but a large bouquet wrapped in white paper, that is what the chambermaid, gloomy where a native of Judea would never be, brings her mistress stripped of every veil, Olympia, whose sovereign indifference seems even crueler than the demented passion with which Salomé burns!

◇

In the morning, in our house in Essone, in the bedroom with two single beds where we're sleeping this winter weekend because there's better heating there than in our usual bedroom, my wife tells me about a nightmare that seemed to her to last a very long time, if not the entire night, and that continues to affect her deeply: with no way of turning back, she stands on a large boulder that's slowly crumbling and that she, terrified, knows will soon crack completely and give way under her feet.

This dream—doubly realistic because, on the one hand, nothing takes place in it that isn't more or less plausible and, on the other, it corresponds fairly directly to our situation as people whose life expectancy has significantly decreased and who worry more than ever about the terrible turn that was recently taken by the current events we are informed of by newspapers, radio, and television—I could have dreamed myself.

Coming from my wife, who is ordinarily inclined to tease me for my tendency to see the dark side of things, the bleak character of this dream was a surprise. Could some kind of telepathic phenomenon, abolishing the space between our two beds and establishing itself in absolute silence between us without any intervening communicating gesture, could that have led her to take my place in the anxious dream that I didn't have? Or should I take this only as the index of a convergence of our two minds, which are consumed by the same heavy worries and which two days prior had mourned the first anniversary of the death of someone who had been very close to us? The hypothesis that does not include the supernatural is obviously the simplest one, and that is enough for me to prefer it to the other. Whatever its cause, it pains me to observe that a shadow has cast itself over my companion whose clear and beautiful courage in the face of transitions large or small, which has always been a soothing counterpoint to my sad lack of bravery, now seems (motif of remorse) to have been overtaken by my pessimism—after the opposite having prevailed for so long—unless (motif of fear) planetary affairs along with our own have in fact turned so dark that, for her as much as for myself, the sun will never shine again.

Which is not her fault, but because I am accustomed to her being the saving grace that silences my alarms, I am tortuously driven to scold her for it!

◇

When speaking or writing that tenderly feminine name that had become the only means he had of reestablishing a semblance of contact with the person he had lost, it was as if his mind had no other syllable at its disposal and as if—deprived almost as much as Baudelaire had been when at the end of his life his vocabulary was limited, according to his biographers, to "God damn!"—he had only that name's well-trodden path to connect him with the outside world.

Ribbon that's pitch dark but that helps you see clearly.
Ribbon whose jade black seems to resist oblivion's eraser.
Ribbon that, despite its gadfly airs, is the lash of a whip.
Ribbon that makes you tasteful, not trashy.
Ribbon that life's crudeness calls for like a seasoning.
Ribbon that, although formal, is for everyday wear.
Ribbon that's the best deal even though it's the most expensive.
Ribbon you must learn to tie and not abandon to the wind.
Ribbon that exerts its charm right where it tightens at your throat.
Ribbon you must roll and unroll, until one thing leads to another. . .

◇

In a nondescript but constructed spot, a very clean, stripped-down and "functional" place, in the full geometric light of what most likely is a summer day, I find myself curled nearly into a ball on the edge of a tall rectangular opening (like a door or a window without a screen) on a completely indefinite void that I know is profound, since its ground is invisible, if it even exists. The temptation to throw myself across the narrow opening to the other side is strong; to escape, through an act that would require no physical effort, the interminable anxiety from which I see no other means of deliverance left. And yet I give up on the idea at the very moment when I have more or less decided upon it, since my fear of the sickening fall into the absolute neutrality of the void overtakes my desire to quit.

Wouldn't it be better, the final alternative being so dire, to hold on a little longer rather than slip into that place where, with no possible chance of a reprieve, time's ribbon is cut cleaner than with a razor?

A morning dream, as pathetic as the majority of my awakenings and pre-awakenings have become, where afterwards it takes some time for me to drag myself out of the mire. . . I should add, also, that this dream—an imagined transposition to a miserable reality—and the efforts I made afterwards to tell the story without error or blunder provided me, single-handedly, with a relative and temporary deliverance. A nightmare that can be narrated is certainly preferable to an equally nightmarish idea that, assaulting you without a figure to describe or decrypt, can of course be thought—coldly produced, delivered in its naked cynicism—but not retold!

◇

The fear of looking like someone who, after a history of being an agnostic, became a turncoat *in extremis*, or an impenitent dilettante trying to appear as such *post mortem*, is mostly what keeps me from hoping that my burial is accompanied by the sounds of a beautiful *Requiem* (Mozart's or Verdi's, in particular). If it weren't for this fear, it would please me to affirm, by that diffusion of pre-recorded music—since an actual performance would be out of the question for someone with neither the means nor the desire for a nabob's funeral—that art, as limited as the faith one may have in it may be, continues to mean something even in the presence of death. No other composition that is marked by pure passion (in the style of Puccini, for example) or better yet, by lightness (some charming piece of opera buffa) could be more demonstrative than the deliberately funereal work that a *Requiem* is; hence it is never circumstantial, but simply proves that beyond every pious travesty of his condition that is so difficult to face, man is able, through industry alone, to inject into his precarious existence a touch of the marvelous. But, far from serving the litigious cause of art, wouldn't that suggest that the choice of such an accompaniment is nothing other than the fruit of an idle desire for provocation?

$\diamond$

The presence of neither the stranger that *Olympia* remains, nor Victorine Meurent, nor even the prestigious Édouard Manet but—more curiously—a figure who, before somehow being baptized *Olympia*, was painted by Édouard Manet with the help of Victorine Meurent, whose charms found a mirror (faithful or not) on that canvas where something that had never existed before appeared.

I know an abstract painter whose devotion to his art is not without a certain heroism (working at night despite being exhausted by days sacrificed to the most thankless tasks). Still young, he is—according to the gossip of a mutual friend—the son of a professional striptease artist, an art that exceeds the figurative because it involves showing in all its radiance, at the conclusion of a rite calculated to arouse impatience and in which one person is both idol and servant, the seductive reality of a female body.

Wouldn't withdrawing, as much as he could, from every observable reality, and avoiding the presence of anything that an image might invoke, be for the artist in question a radical means of encountering nothing that, on his canvas, would directly or indirectly remind him of the nudity to which a shameful career condemned (or still condemns) his mother?

As for myself, a writer of completely bourgeois parentage, not only do I work first and foremost with immediate realities, but I readily proceed from there to a sort of mental striptease. I have, in fact, no fear of implicating—by extension—someone to whom I owe congenital respect that would conflict with laying myself bare (revealing myself to the maximum or, if necessary, telling the naked truth), an act that is limited only by these two other fears: of lapsing into banal platitudes or revealing my flaws too explicitly, flaws that are greater and heavier than what my seemingly unrestrained remarks might suggest.

◇

Dream not dreamt:

At the risk of falling into the abyss, the hell of today's world (murder, deceit, tortures, burials, famines), I must travel from one end to the other of a tightrope that, at a very high altitude, forms the letters of the alphabet. Using my two hands to hold on and with my legs dangling in the void, I move from one letter to the next, seized with nausea each time that, in order to move a step forward, I must let go of one of my hands, not without hesitation, and venture towards the next letter. Starting from A, I wonder if I will have the strength to make it to Z, where I know that—like a tightrope walker reaching his platform after a difficult crossing—I will be safe. My desire to give up is strong, because of vertigo as much as the absurdity of my situation, but what to do? If I decide to give up, I will have to actually do it or go back to the beginning, an undertaking that is just as perilous as the first, or stay hanging on the consonant or the vowel beyond which I'm unable to continue my precarious advance.

◇

Art:
baroque proliferation on life's hard edges,
seigneurial luxury,
but château that yields to surging, too-furious
  tempests.

◇

The twofold end I would like to achieve when, seeking firmer ground than pure invention, I orient my work towards realism:

by enacting (albeit within a fictional framework) a living reality, to root the text and give it a density that neither shadow nor dream possess;

to redeem the real, as bleak as it may be, by creating—without cosmetics—a bit of gold out of one of its fragments (or simulacrum of a fragment).

◇

The ribbon that, without strangling her, encircles Olympia's neck and whose knot—a conventional *ad libitum* sign of the infinite, an authenticating signature, or the twinned blades of a propeller that conjure up sensual flights—sets it apart from the serpent that, biting its own tail, illustrates the eternal return, this ribbon that, for me whose double desire for realist exactitude and density does not prevent me from being seduced by the vagaries of analogy, suggests much more than what its strict nature demands, has this ribbon of modest length and width been the thread that has kept me from losing myself completely in the labyrinth that writing has dragged me into, or should I see it only as a trivial afterthought that will eventually wear thin, like the frills of a coquette's dress? Neither Ariadne's thread nor an embellishment, but a string pulled almost on the off chance that it might open a curtain onto a clarity that reveals something I do not expect, I think this ribbon must be seen as the concrete detail that first gave me a foothold and, while in itself as insignificant as a piece of fly-paper on which all sorts of flying insects get stuck, played no less of a motivating role than what the working hypothesis plays for the savant. That the nude painted by Manet (in a painting so conceptually new that it created a scandal in its day) achieves so much truth through such a minor detail, that ribbon that modernizes Olympia and, even more than a beauty mark or a patch of freckles would, renders her more precise and more immediately visible, making her a woman with ties to a particular milieu and era, that is what lends itself to reflection, if not divagation!

Would it demonstrate an idiotically positivist mind to hope that such a detail could enter into an artist or writer's every creation, a detail that, locating and actualizing it, would confer an undeniable realness upon the whole by essentially causing it to crystallize in a reality it would never have possessed if that sturdy fragment hadn't acted as bait? What's more, can the idea you hope to develop be anything more than a dead idea if, at the very start, the ribbon or detail is ruined by the intervening gesture you make to seize it, not as an abstract thing but a bird of prey whose coat or plumage distinguishes it from the rest? Finally, mustn't I know how to capture—day after day—the innumerable trivial incidents that emerge from insipidity when I recount them, in scrupulous historiography and without recourse to spices imported from some foreign land?

Take note, however, that while the joys in question demand training, they cannot be prepared according to trusted recipes, as one might prepare a light meal; handling these joys—the most significant of which are those that, spontaneous reactions to beauty that we grasp in order to transcend the ordinary, seem to prove by their very profundity that everything is completely absurd and thus hope is permissible in many domains—as such would amount to placing them on the same level as the pleasures of the palate that gastronomy provides, undeniably an art, but one that illuminates nothing. Can I treat these glorious moments to which I aspire—in life and, failing that, in writing—as if they were cordon bleu practices to which I had been invited by my deep fascination with the ribbon at the throat of a cold and troubling demoness?

O.K.!

All the same—and this saddens me—that ribbon, whatever value I may attach to it, is only a poor spider's thread, and I wouldn't dream of claiming it to be a humble strand of the noose that could strangle these monsters in multiple forms: racism (which will not admit the evidence that every human is a human being), fascism of all kinds (which despises our species to the point of believing that it must be ruled with an iron fist), and the other ignominies that, although founded on the most hackneyed ideas, seem to be defiling the world more irrevocably with every passing day.

◇

Long ago,
used to be,
once,

yesterday,
today,
tomorrow,

soon,
later,
never.

ABOUT THE AUTHOR

Michel Leiris (1901–1990) was a French surrealist writer and ethnographer. Part of the Surrealist group in Paris, Leiris became a key member of the College of Sociology with Georges Bataille and head of research in ethnography at the CNRS.